AUTHENTIC MANHOOD

DAILY REFLECTIONS FOR MEN

AUTH ENTIC MAN HOOD

Book I

A MAN AND HIS DESIGN

S t e v e   S n i d e r

invite
PRESS

Plano, Texas

Contents

Prologue   xi

Introduction   xiii

Day 1
Masculine Identity Crisis   1

Day 2
Asking for Directions   3

Day 3
Disconnected   5

Day 4
All of Your Heart   7

Day 5
Surpassing Knowledge   9

Day 6
Blueprint   11

Day 7
Vision   13

Day 8
Passion and Purpose   15

Day 9
Don't Just Stuff It   17

Day 10
The Great Escape   19

Day 11
Create and Cultivate   21

Day 12
Courage to Lean   23

Day 13
Initiative   25

Day 14
Our New Self   27

Day 15
The Caretaker   29

Day 16
The Runner   31

Day 17
The Achievement Fix   33

Day 18
The Masked Man   35

Day 19
The Authentic Man   37

Day 20
Seek and Find   39

Day 21
Deep Intimacy   41

Day 22
Positivity Resonance   43

Day 23
The Master Architect   45

Day 24
The Allure of the
Easy Chair   47

Day 25
Fighting Dragons   49

Day 26
My Team   51

Day 27
Investing for the
Long Haul   53

Day 28
Identity   55

Contents

Day 29
Trust and Do Good 59

Day 30
Missing the Mark 61

Day 31
Diamond in the Rough 63

Day 32
Hidden and Isolated 65

Day 33
The Quest for
the Holy Grail 67

Day 34
Heart, Soul, Mind, and
Strength 69

Day 35
A Way to Live 71

Day 36
Strength in Humility 73

Day 37
Crippling Doubt 75

Day 38
Seeing and Healing 77

Day 39
The Shadow 79

Day 40
No Victims Allowed 81

Day 41
The Heart of a Man 83

Day 42
Skipping Rocks 85

Day 43
The Art of Painting 87

Day 44
Be Grateful 89

Day 45
The Need for Connection 91

Day 46
The Secret Power of
Affirmation 93

Day 47
The Consumer 95

Day 48
The Expert 97

Day 49
The Pause 99

Day 50
Living in Community 101

Day 51
Love Letters to God 103

Day 52
Reverse Engineering 105

Day 53
The Path 107

Day 54
What Can I Do for You? 109

Day 55
Grief Transformation 111

Day 56
The Season of Spring 113

Day 57
The Season of Summer 115

Day 58
The Season of Fall 117

Day 59
The Season of Winter 119

Day 60
A Life-Giving Spirit 121

*To my sweet, kind, beautiful
and wonderful wife Beth,*

I love you!

PROLOGUE

In the year 2000, *Sports Illustrated* identified what they believed to be "The Century's Greatest Sports Photos." Dozens of photos were in the running, many that remain famous today because of the epic moments they capture. The finalists included pictures of sports icons like Muhammad Ali, Michael Jordan, Willie Mays, Secretariat, Jackie Robinson, and others in some of their finest moments.

The photo they chose as the greatest of the century surprised the entire world. The winner took you inside the Texas Christian University (TCU) football locker room minutes before the team was to take the field in the 1957 Cotton Bowl to play against Syracuse University and, many would say, the best running back of all time, the great Jim Brown.

What you see is the entire team sitting in their lockers with the coach standing in the middle of the room, presumably sharing his final thoughts before they took the field. Each of the boys are staring into space, serious looks on their faces, clearly anticipating what's to come. The accompanying article said it's as if they'd entered a deep tunnel together.

In sharing why they picked this photo out of all the other greats, *Sports Illustrated* explained that this one invited you into something deeper than the others, into a place that . . .

most folks go maybe once or twice in a lifetime, when their mamas or daddies die or their children are born, a place they don't go nearly as often as they should. It invites you into a room of ... men about to go to war... The older you get, the more you realize that **THIS** is what sports are most about; the moments **BEFORE**, the times when a person takes **a flashlight to his soul** and inspects himself for will and courage and spirit, the stuff that separates men such as Jordan and Ali from the rest more than anything in their forearms or their fingers or their feet. **Who am I?** And **is that going to be enough?**

Maybe you've sat in a locker room yourself before a big moment, feeling deeply in your soul exactly what those TCU football players were feeling. Maybe another experience in life has caused you to inspect yourself and get clear and focused. Or maybe you've never gone deep into your core and looked at what's going on in your soul.

Seizing these moments and asking these big questions are crucial parts of any man's journey toward authentic manhood. They shape who we are, how we live, and the ultimate results we get.

At some point, many of us leave sports and other similar pursuits behind, and we head into life without creating these important, character-shaping and faith-building moments. Moments that shape who we are in our marriage, our job, our fatherhood, our relationships and other major areas of our life ... moments in which we pause, ponder and reflect on the things that matter most ... moments when we ask the big questions, like, "Who am I? Am I enough? And who do I desire to become?"

May these *Daily Reflections* be a tool for taking a flashlight to your soul, connecting deeply with God, and shaping who you are as a man.

INTRODUCTION

Become the Man You Were Created to Be

This is one of six books of daily reflections especially crafted for men. Today more than ever, we men need a sense of identity and direction. We need positive encouragement. We need healthy ways to relieve stress in our lives, to find meaningful spiritual sustenance, and to anchor ourselves in practical wisdom.

The wisdom offered here is drawn foundationally from scripture. It also contains a few nuggets I've learned or unlearned through the years. Some of it is inspired by the related video resource *33 The Series*.

I've written these daily reflections to myself and for myself as much as I have for you. They help me pause, ponder, and reflect on some of the things that matter most in life.

Hopefully, these reflections will be a helpful guide for you as you journey into what I'll call "authentic manhood." That doesn't mean perfect manhood. Quite the opposite. It means honest manhood. For me and many others around the globe, it means a Christ-centered manhood. To pursue authentic manhood means to be on a journey to discover and be your real self . . . a journey to know your self and to know God . . . a journey to be who God made you to be. Mistakes and all. Bad decisions and good. Strengths and weaknesses. If you let Him, God uses it all.

These reflections will draw you into some of men's deepest struggles, biggest questions, and some of our greatest fears, joys, and needs. Hopefully, you'll find them thought provoking, spiritually encouraging, and heartfelt. Each one will ask probing questions for you to process the daily issues you're facing in your relationships, workplace, and home.

Go beyond just reading the words. Sit in them. Contemplate the meaning of each reflection in your own life. Ask if it helps reveal anything about yourself you need to hear. Maybe you'll see something about yourself you haven't seen before. As you experience any meaningful moments, invite God in. Invite Him in to both the good and the bad. Meet Him in the depths of your soul. For me, that's where real transformation seems to begin.

Why direct these reflections toward men? While men and women have much in common, there are some unique differences beyond just the physical. I've discovered in three decades of working with men that it is deeply meaningful to talk to men about manhood . . . to encourage them in their manhood journey with all of its challenges, opportunities, questions, and uncertainties.

My hope and prayer is that these daily reflections will be helpful as you shape your own unique manhood journey. That they'll help you be more self-aware and Christ-centered. That they may be a guide to you, a solace, an inspiration. And that they'll be a resource to help you ponder life and nourish your soul.

Tips for Getting the Most Out of This Book

GET A JOURNAL Be sure you have a journal that you can write in.

1. PERSONALIZE YOUR JOURNEY. Each reflection ends with an Action Step as well as some reflection questions. Be sure to set aside time for these. Your journal is the perfect place to record your responses and personalize your journey.

2. GET OUT OF YOUR HEAD. Allow the reflections to take you into your heart. We men already tend to spend a lot of time in our heads. Allow the reflections be like a flashlight shining brightly into the depths of your soul. See what's going on in there . . . maybe see some things you haven't seen in a while.

3. GO THROUGH IT WITH SOME BUDDIES. After going through the reflections personally, consider going through them with a group of guys. Enjoy encouraging each other and growing together. Let the reflections be a prompt to go deep with other guys.

4. SHARE IT WITH THE IMPORTANT WOMEN IN YOUR LIFE. While the reflections are directed toward men, share them with the women in your life who love you. Invite them into the struggles, questions, fears, joys, and needs of men. It might just stimulate some great conversations!

5. GO THROUGH THE *33 THE SERIES* VIDEO RESOURCE. Grab a group of guys and go through *33 The Series* together, a six-volume video series that gives men a Christ-centered vision of manhood. It gives you manhood tracks to run on and sets you up to create meaningful community with other men. It would be a great accompaniment to these reflections.

A Man and His Design

An important distinction before we begin: "Conventional Manhood" vs. "Authentic Manhood"

- Men were designed for a unique purpose. The quest for that purpose defines the man you will become. Your quest begins with discovering who you are and who you were created to be.

- Many men lack confidence in their masculinity and aren't sure what it means to be a man in today's culture. How can you cultivate a compelling and authentic vision of what it means to be a man in today's world? This is a primary question that will accompany you on this journey as you shape that vision for yourself. As we shape vision, it's helpful to have a model of AUTHENTIC MANHOOD. For me, the model is Jesus. His way is the way that will guide our journey together.

- CONVENTIONAL MANHOOD, on the other hand, teaches men to be consumers rather than cultivators. A consumer mentality allows you to believe that the world exists primarily for your pleasure, comfort, and entertainment. But this is a false illusion that will lead you into a place of superficiality and a lack of fulfillment, affecting your work, your relationships, and your legacy.

- Most men are fixers by nature. Learning that we can't fix ourselves by ourselves is an important part of our journey toward AUTHENTIC MANHOOD. We need others. We need relationships with other men we can trust. Trusted relationships with God and others can help us heal the deep-seated wounds we carry around in our hearts that keep us chained to a consumer mentality.

- Your consumer mentality sets you up for traps that will bring you down in all areas of your life. Your search for authenticity will help you recognize those traps and veer away from them toward a more fulfilling and meaningful life.

- Men who are pursuing AUTHENTIC MANHOOD are doing their best to reject passivity, accept responsibility, lead courageously, and invest eternally in the important areas of life. They are desiring to live a life of meaning, passion, and purpose that makes a positive difference in the world and is a blessing to others.

MASCULINE IDENTITY CRISIS

What does it mean to be a man? Today, that's not an easy answer. Hollywood has given us some popular images of manhood in the movies: the tough, isolated, misunderstood hero, the big, strong, handsome stud, the cool, chill, heartthrob, and the reckless, rebellious, risk-taker. None of these seem to work long term in everyday life.

These images have perpetuated an idea of manhood in which men must push their emotions aside and attempt to appear in command and in control at all times . . . to have it all together. Men who have bought into this kind of definition often feel a deep sense of loneliness and despair, or they default to acting out their stuffed-up feelings in passive-aggressive ways. This can quickly get out of hand.

Current culture describes over-the-top toughness as "toxic masculinity," defined by men who exhibit dominance, control, or anti-feminist behavior to assert power over women and others. Most of us can agree, this is not an image we want to identify with.

We don't want to be wimps, unable to defend our families and lead in our workplaces. But we also don't want to be overbearing, controlling, or dominant. The truth is, many of us don't know how to act, because we don't know who we are. We have lost sight of our identity.

So, who are we? Is there such a thing as a masculine identity? How can we embrace our masculinity and yet be relational, kind, approachable, and secure in who we are? How can we protect our family, stand up for what is right, and pursue our goals while still remaining connected, open, and tender-hearted?

Imagine your manhood in a way that both strengthens your masculine identity and also allows you to be vulnerable and engageable. A masculinity that allows you to be strong in maybe some new kinds of ways—to be comfortable in your own skin, to reveal your faults with honesty, and to maximize your strengths for the benefit of others with humility and grace.

This kind of authenticity is possible, but it takes introspection, emotional maturity, courage, and work. And it also takes having someone you can follow. Someone who models it for you. Jesus is my model and my inspiration for authentic manhood. The way of authentic manhood is the way of Jesus.

— ACTION STEP —

Write in your journal what you think it means to be a man in today's world. Write down how you would describe your own masculine identity.

What kind of images have informed my vision of manhood? How would those close to me describe me as a man and how I live out my manhood? How do I balance masculinity with relationality in a way that feels authentic and real?

ASKING FOR DIRECTIONS

You know the old joke. Instead of asking for directions or getting out the map, most men will veer into an uncharted direction. We are determined to go our own way, sure that our "brave," lone path will lead us to our destination.

This inclination has been cultivated in our bones since we were born. We are encouraged to be self-sufficient, independent, daring, and bold. Any sense of need or reliance on others has been mislabeled as weak at best or deficient at worst. And so, we charge ahead, often with no direction and no assistance.

We can be guilty of doing this same thing with our life, trying to go it alone. And we can find ourselves lost in the woods, aimless and confused with life.

Aimless and confused men create problems for both themselves and others. They usually end up seeking alternative and unhealthy ways of redirecting the pain and loneliness they are feeling.

When we're aimless and confused, we can easily be redirected toward easy grabs. These easy grabs may make us feel victorious for the moment. But in fact, they are traps. Like quicksand, they suck us down further into our aimlessness and pain.

Some of us end up with unhealthy addictions. Some of us may bury ourselves in work. Some may go the route of sex addiction or pornography. Some may resort to anger and violence, affairs, or other adolescent behaviors.

When you feel aimless and confused, what do you do? Do you try to go it alone? Do you turn to other avenues to satisfy your need for purpose and meaning?

The way of Jesus is to do life together, not to walk our paths alone. He modeled that with his twelve disciples. They did life together. They carried each other's burdens. Only when you admit you cannot go your road alone and are willing to ask for directions can you truly begin to walk the path of authentic manhood . . . a path that leads you to a life of meaning, passion, and purpose.

— ACTION STEP —

Write in your journal the ways you react when you feel lost or confused. It's helpful to see those things in writing. Reflect on what it is that makes you respond as you do.

Where in my life do I feel aimless and confused? What am I wrestling with? What would it take for me to ask someone else for help? Who are the friends or mentors in my life who are walking my path with me?

DISCONNECTED

We men love to fix things. So, it's no great surprise that when something seems broken in our lives, our first inclination is to "fix it." When we aren't sure how to proceed, we often will "disconnect" from the problem until we can figure out a way to fix it that makes sense to us.

Unfortunately, when it comes to brokenness in relationships, our "disconnects" often put us in hot water. They can be experienced by our families and friends as disinterest, which can cause friction. And then, when things seem to be heating up instead of cooling off, what do we do? We disconnect more. Sometimes, we entirely disengage. To us, this makes perfect sense. To others, it can be hurtful and frustrating.

Why do we do this? While some of it may be due to our simple desire to fix things, this often has its roots in something bigger and deeper—maybe it's that, as men, we're just not willing to admit our confusion or lack of direction about a problem. Or, we feel the need to solve everything by ourselves in order to be respected real men.

Many men have been raised with an idea of masculinity that has the potential to alienate and isolate us in the times that we most need help. Instead of reaching out when we don't know how to deal with a relational issue, we cut the line, disconnect, and try to figure it all out on our own.

To live more authentically in relationship with others, we need to put aside our impulse to "fix" everything ourselves and allow ourselves the grace to be human, the freedom to be sometimes confused, and even the permission to fail.

— ACTION STEP —

Recall in your journal times you've chosen to disconnect rather than draw near in some of your close relationships. How could you have handled those instances in more helpful and healing ways?

When things are broken in a relationship, am I more likely to "disconnect" or to draw near so we can work on it together? How can I get better at staying connected to my family and friends even when things go wrong?

ALL OF YOUR HEART

Feelings can emerge in our lives that we don't know what to do with. If we bottle up and bury these feelings, we can begin to become numb. A lot of us have been conditioned to push through our feelings, to persevere through the pain, or worse, to ignore it completely.

But our feelings are telling us something important about ourselves. God gave us feelings to tell us what is going on in our heart. And Jesus calls us to love God with ALL of our heart. But only if we know what's going on in our heart can we give it ALL to Him.

What's going on in YOUR heart? What are you feeling?

Hurt? Fear? Sadness? Loneliness? Gladness? Anger? Shame?

Become aware of what is going on in your heart so you can give it ALL to God. And also so you can share your heart with your family and close friends. It's when we bring things into the light that we can heal. It's when we turn over everything in our heart to God that we can enjoy His peace and true freedom.

Scripture gives us some helpful guidance in giving our heart to God:

- Jesus models this for us when He shares the sorrow in His heart with His disciples the night before His crucifixion. He modeled it again later that night when He cried out in tears to His Father, sharing every emotion He must have been feeling in that moment of desperation (Mark 14:34-36).

- God can deliver us from our fears if we take them to Him (Psalm 34).

- The apostle Paul encourages us to take our confusion and anxiety to God so we can enjoy a peace that comes from Him (Philippians 4:6-7).

- We're told that when we turn to Christ, He can remove the veil that covers our heart so we can enjoy the freedom He offers to those who seek Him (2 Corinthians 3:16-18).

It can take some courage to be honest about what's going on in your heart. But one of the greatest gifts you can give to yourself is to let yourself feel your feelings, be able to share them in your close relationships, and be able to give ALL of your heart to God.

— ACTION STEP —

Reflect on what is going on in your heart. Become aware of what you are feeling. Don't rush it; give it some time. If you've buried your feelings over time, it can take some time and space to even be aware of what they are. Invite God into them with you. Give Him ALL of your heart.

Am I willing to look deeply and honestly into my heart and share what's in there with the Lord? Both the good and the bad? Am I willing to get it out into the light for healing by sharing it with a trusted friend?

Day Five

SURPASSING KNOWLEDGE

The apostle Paul prays in his letter to the Ephesians that the people would receive God's Spirit in their inner being so that Christ might dwell in their hearts through faith . . . and that they would know the love of God in a way that surpasses knowledge (Ephesians 3:16-19).

It seems to me that Paul is praying for a transformation. He's praying that Christ might dwell inside them . . . and that they may know His love so deeply that it "surpasses knowledge."

Much of my personal faith journey has been focused on gaining knowledge about God . . . learning about Him . . . knowing everything scripture says about Him . . . being able to defend both Him and my faith in Him. My journey was heavily focused on having all the right answers about God. Of course, there is nothing wrong with pursuing knowledge. I'm all for knowing as much about God as we are capable of knowing.

But Paul seems to be talking about something different and maybe even deeper than just knowledge *about* God. He prays for a comprehension that comes from inside . . . from God's Spirit in us. A comprehension of the love of Christ that "fills us with the fullness" of God.

9

As you pray for and seek this for yourself, allow His Spirit to take you beyond your knowledge of God and into your heart, where Christ dwells. Knowledge is wonderful but is limited. Paul is giving us a glimpse of a love that exceeds knowledge . . . the love of Christ that fills us with the fullness of God . . . a love that changes everything we think about manhood.

— ACTION STEP —

Pray Paul's prayer for yourself, that you may experience this love.

Are you filled with the fullness of God? Do you enjoy His goodness in your inner being?

BLUEPRINT

Every man has been given a general blueprint for his life. Many men aren't aware of this and others have simply lost sight of it. But, as a man, you have been created with a unique blueprint.

The Genesis creation story tells us that we were created by God in His image. You were made to be, like God, a creator and a cultivator. You were designed to create and to then cultivate what you create. So a major part of your manhood journey is to discover what your creation projects will be and how they will serve others. And then to cultivate those creations so they are healthy and meaningful and cared for.

To create doesn't mean you have to be an artist or a builder. There are many ways to create. Your blueprint could be to create in any number of ways. It could be to create farms that grow food; to create houses for people to live in; to create experiences that bless others; to create teams that compete for championships; to create roads for people to travel on; to create ministry activities that serve others; to create business deals that help companies thrive; to create services that assist people; to create art or entertainment for others to appreciate; or to create wonderful meals for others to enjoy. You get the point.

You were made in the image of God to create and cultivate for the benefit of others. That's part of your responsibility as a man.

Again, that will look different for every man, but we were all made and given that blueprint as an important part of our lives. And, by the way, that blueprint gives you purpose, which every man needs in his life. We all need meaning and purpose in our lives.

You personally have unique, internal gifts to use in order to fulfill your blueprint. Identifying your gifts and skills and finding ways to craft a life according to God's blueprint for you will bring a deep satisfaction to your life. It will help you live a life of meaning, passion, and purpose.

— ACTION STEP —

If you're not clear about your purpose, about what you were made to create in your life, take some steps toward knowing that. Ask close friends when do they see you at your best. Take personality inventories like YOUR UNIQUE DESIGN or STRENGTHSFINDER to give you helpful feedback. This is an important part of your manhood journey. Take a step.

What am I doing to use my God-given gifts and abilities to fulfill God's blueprint for my life? What do I have to offer to the world that no one else can? What can I create that gives meaning to my life and blesses others?

Day Seven

VISION

A man's life needs to be filled with vision, passion, and purpose. But everything starts with vision. Proverbs 29:18 says that without a clear vision, people perish. Lack of clarity about who you are and what you care about can leave you feeling aimless and unmotivated.

You don't need to have everything in life figured out in advance, but you do need to have a vision for your future. You need to have direction for your life. You need to know:

- who you are and who you want to become;

- what kind of life goals you're aiming for; and

- the kind of relationships you value and are willing to commit to.

Vision provides direction, focus, energy, and endurance to stay the course even in the face of difficulty and change. A man committed to a clear vision will be much more likely to pursue it despite obstacles. His vision allows him to see what's possible so he can draw on his resources and take the steps to live it.

A man who has a clear vision can inspire others. A man who knows where he is going can lead others to follow. He can become a positive difference-maker.

Seeing is not the same as vision. You can see things but still not know where you are going. Part of the journey to authentic manhood is having a clear vision of where you're going and of who you want to be as a man.

— ACTION STEP —

Write in your journal a vision for each of the different areas of your life: family life, work life, social life, spiritual life. Identify steps that will move you toward your vision in the next month, the next six months, the next year. Pray that as you plan your way, the Lord will guide your steps.

What is the vision for my life? Who do I want to be? What things, people, or ideas are most important to me? In what or in whom is my vision rooted? How does my vision give my life meaning and purpose?

Day Eight
PASSION AND PURPOSE

Men who love something will invest in it with heart and soul. Passion ensures purpose and purpose ignites passion. Once your vision is in place and you know where you want to go and who you want to be, you're more likely to get excited about your prospects, your future, and where you're headed.

I know when I get most excited about my vision and my purpose is when I feel a peace that it is from God. Knowing that I've searched the scripture and gone to God in prayer to seek His guidance. Sometimes I feel it and sometimes I don't. But when I do, it's like wind in my sails and it ignites me to act on it. Acting on our vision provides us with purpose.

Think of preparing, cleaning, and readying your boat for the open waters. Boats take a lot of work. They require a huge investment of time, energy, and resources. What drives that work and commitment? It's the vision. The vision of sailing on the open waters with the wind in your hair and the sun on your face. It's seeing the smiles and hearing the laughter of others you will be inviting to join you. That boat has become part of your vision and reflects something about your passion and purpose. You are passionate about sailing. You want to enjoy sailing and sharing that with others. It makes you feel alive and fulfilled.

The same goes for your life. When your vision includes passion and purpose and involves serving others, you're going to be likely to invest yourself in it to make it come true.

Cultivating vision, passion, and purpose for your life is really important. As you do so, take it to the Lord and seek His guidance. Proverbs 16:9 reminds us that the heart of a man plans his way but the Lord directs his steps. I love the idea of pouring my heart into a clear vision of purpose and seeking the Lord to direct my steps.

— ACTION STEP —

Put in writing your dreams of living a life of passion and purpose. Pray that the Lord will direct your steps.

What vision am I investing in? What dreams or endeavors ignite my sense of passion and purpose? Do I feel a peace that my vision is from God?

DON'T JUST STUFF IT

When things go wrong in our lives, or when stress rears its head, it's easy to fall into that age-old, conventional male response: just stuff it! Just push it down, out of mind and out of sight. We refuse to feel the anxiety and the pain because it can make us feel helpless, afraid, vulnerable, and confused . . . out of control and out of our comfort zone.

It's tempting to simply go on with your life, pretending that nothing is wrong. You opt to get hyperfocused on your work at hand or engage in activities that will distract you from the gnawing worry or pain. You convince yourself that you can't give in to the powerful emotions that are welling up inside.

Stuffing is exactly that—it's your attempt to stuff powerful emotions into a little box and stow it somewhere deep inside and out of the way . . . somewhere you can pretend it doesn't exist . . . somewhere you imagine it can't affect you.

Strong emotions can feel overwhelming. They can make you feel out of control. They can make you worry that you will be overcome by them if you don't stuff them, that somehow, they will destroy your sense of equilibrium.

In fact, the opposite is true. Stuffing creates a kind of time-bomb that ticks below the surface for a period of time. But the pressure always wins in the end. Someday, when you least expect it, those feelings will begin to erupt in terrible kinds of ways. You may lash out at a co-worker or your family over something totally unrelated. You may become snappy, distracted, and unfocused, because all of your energy is consumed in trying to hold down that powder keg. You may even become depressed and exhausted and resort to harmful activities that threaten your relationships, your work, your health, and even your life.

Think of trying to hold down a buoy for an extended time while treading water. Stuffing is an exhausting activity. Instead, if you allow yourself to feel your pain, your wounds, your feelings of despair, it may not be pleasant for the moment, but you will find yourself letting go of the buoy. You allow it to float to the surface, bobbing up and down on the water, serving its proper purpose.

Allow your feelings and emotions to serve their proper purpose. God created us to be feeling creatures. Be authentic with yourself and those close to you by seeing and holding and sharing your true feelings and emotions. Allow your feelings to show you what you are needing. Allow them to point you to your need to meet God in them . . . to invite God into them with you. Offer them to Jesus in prayer. Give them to Him. Experiencing the love and grace of Jesus in the midst of your feelings is refreshingly healing and freeing.

— ACTION STEP —

Create some quiet time and space and journal about what you are feeling. Be honest with yourself. Give yourself some time to see your feelings and be aware of them. Then close your eyes and invite God to meet you in them.

Do I stuff things down when I feel stressed or upset? How do I act out my feelings and emotions? How can I stop stuffing and give myself permission to recognize and feel my feelings? Am I willing to listen to what my feelings are telling me about me?

THE GREAT ESCAPE

When a man finds that he can't *stuff* his feelings and his unresolved pain begins finding ways to seep out and sabotage his life, he will then often try the second conventional male response: the great *escape*.

The great escape is based on a lie. When a man falls into this belief system, he can come to believe that, like his favorite super hero, he is invincible and untouchable. He can also find less than wise ways to escape what haunts him. He believes that if he keeps on running, his emotions will never catch up to him. He doesn't realize that they are always the monkey on his back, and that monkey, when not acknowledged, can be rather mischievous.

Our escapes can turn into unhealthy addictions. Some men may get lost in excessive gaming or non-stop sports. Others may escape into alcoholism, drugs, or pornography. Some men overwork and spend every waking minute at the office. Others go on the road and keep moving until they run out of gas. If we're honest, we've all been tempted by some means of escape. But escapes can never last. Sooner or later, the adventure ends and reality sets in. The more dynamic the escapes, the more uninviting reality appears until a man is living a virtual life. He has become a mere shell of his former existence.

No man is invincible to pain. Life comes with all kinds of experiences, feelings, joys, and pains. To live life really, fully, and authentically, you have to engage with it. You have to learn to see your pain and your feelings as gifts that are telling you something really important about yourself. Telling you where you've been hurt and what you need from others and from God. The more you engage, the more you will discover that your true strength lies not in invincibility but in transparency and authenticity. That's where real growth and maturity and transformation can begin to take place.

— ACTION STEP —

Take a brave step today. Let go of something you are holding on to in an attempt to escape your feelings and your pain. Share that you've taken this step with someone close to you.

What ways do I try to escape my feelings? How can I break this unhealthy pattern? How can I more fully engage with myself, my work, my wife, and my friends? Why am I so afraid of a pain that could be telling me something really important about myself?

Day Eleven

CREATE AND CULTIVATE

Whether you describe yourself as a painter, a bricklayer, a carpenter, an electrician, a guitarist, a dancer, a coach, a businessman, a pianist, a doctor, a plumber, or something else, you more than likely learned your trade and developed much of your skill with the help of someone who excelled in their field.

In the same way, when it comes to living our lives, we as men are called to model ourselves after a Master of Life . . . God, the creator of the heavens and the earth, of the stars and fields, water and seeds, clouds and leaves. And then, after creating, He cultivated. He cultivated what He had created with a plethora of "good" things. Then He invited man into the picture to help Him in His continued work of creating and cultivating our world.

Men, we were born with a mission—to create and to cultivate. We were created specifically in God's likeness, made in His image, so that we would have the creativity, the faculty, the ability, and the passion to create good things and then to cultivate them so that they flourish. These "good things" don't have to be physical things. They can be relational or spiritual or cultural or social or supportive or artistic things. We were created to be life-givers to the world. That's quite a vision and quite a purpose! It's God's vision and purpose for every single one of us.

God sent us the ultimate example of how to live out this purpose. He sent Jesus, who showed us what it means to create good in our world and to then cultivate it in love.

— ACTION STEP —

Make a list of good things you've created in your lifetime and then ask yourself if you've cultivated them well. Consider what good God has put you on earth to create.

How can I live out my identity as an apprentice of the Creator, having been made in His likeness? In what ways can I create and cultivate in my daily life? How can I live my life in a way that serves and benefits others?

COURAGE TO LEAN

Many men love to lead. Some were born to lead. But sometimes, that makes it hard for them to *lean*. In an attempt to avoid feeling "needy" or "weak," many men refuse to lean on or rely on anyone else. We can resort to dealing with our problems, dilemmas, or decisions alone. We resist sharing our dreams, ideas, and hopes with others. Too many of us believe that the need to rely on someone else for something is for the girls. This false belief has left generations of men unable to connect emotionally and intimately in relationships with others, whether it be their male friends or the women in their lives.

Authentic men lean. They realize that in allowing themselves to feel vulnerable, to share the deepest parts of themselves, to admit they don't have every answer, to discuss and make decisions with others, is life-giving. It allows them the freedom to be human and it actually strengthens their sense of self. It provides them the confidence and support they need to stand tall in the face of challenge.

When we learn to feel comfortable leaning on God and others for support, encouragement, identity, and stability, we gain a humility and a resilience that makes us strong enough to face anything in life. Leaning on God and other people relieves us of the overbearing responsibility of figuring out everything in life on our own. It relieves us from needing to stuff or escape our pain.

We can place our hope in a Master who has shown His love for us, a love that we can see with our own eyes if we'll just look around. We can enjoy one of the great gifts of life, deep relationships and the love and support of good friends . . . friends who help us celebrate the good in life and endure the storms that come our way.

May we stop glorifying the idea that we should be able to handle everything on our own and start honoring our need to be supported.

— ACTION STEP —

Identify an area of your life where you need someone to lean on . . . you need their strength, their faith, their patience, their experience. Take the initiative to reach out to the right person and . . . lean . . . create the relational connection you need with them.

Do I feel sometimes that I must be self-sufficient to be strong? Do I hold back from leaning on my friends and family for emotional support and nurturing when I truly need it? How can I learn to lean on God in my life as my master and mentor, so I can enjoy the freedom to be vulnerable and authentic with others?

INITIATIVE

In the Book of Genesis, a rather assertive serpent tempts Adam's wife, Eve, with a pernicious lie. He and Eve believe the serpent's lie that God is holding out on them, unwilling to give them the best fruit of the garden. He tells them that if they eat that fruit, they will become independent and powerful just like God. The temptation of self-sufficiency sounds like a great deal to Adam and Eve. Eve steps forward and takes the first bite. Adam follows.

Adam's role in this garden scenario boggles our minds. Why is Adam so passive? Why is he allowing this shifty serpent to con his wife? Instead of Adam stepping in and challenging the serpent, he stands idly by and watches, then allows her to take the first bite. He blandly follows suit. Adam believes he can find his greatest joy by going around God instead of to God. Then he hides.

Lack of initiative often results when we become so intent on not trusting God that we completely disengage. It results when we have a confused sense of our purpose. Like Adam, we allow bad things to happen because we don't want to get involved. We don't trust, we disengage, and that just breeds selfish passivity.

An authentic man takes the initiative to stand up for what is right, to resist what is wrong, and to engage with threats, injustices, and aggression. He takes the initiative to stand up for his wife and protect her from physical, emotional, and spiritual harm.

He places his faith and his hope in the God who created him and seeks strength from Him to resist the lies. He's not tricked by the temptation to face life alone.

Initiative is a paradox. The more we depend on God for our strength, the stronger we become and the more initiative we're prepared to take on behalf of others.

— ACTION STEP —

Identify an area of your life where you aren't fully trusting God. Take the initiative to move toward Him in that place of doubt and seek His strength, pray for His wisdom, and trust in His love for you.

How can I take more initiative for the benefit of others in my life? Do I run to God and trust in His love or do I find myself running around Him and trusting more in my way than His way?

Day Fourteen

OUR NEW SELF

Are you the same person all the time? Do you change who
you are around different people? How do you act when you're
stressed and under pressure? Our true character shines through
when life hits us in the face with unexpected obstacles and difficult challenges.

Sportswriter Heywood Hale Broun noted that "sports don't
build character; they reveal it." Real life can do the same. Who do
you want to be as life reveals who you really are?

For those of us who have chosen to follow the way of Jesus,
the apostle Paul gives us a really compelling vision of who we are
to be when life reveals who we really are. He tells us in Colossians
3:12-15 to put on:

- A COMPASSIONATE HEART. Care for people. Really care
  about and want to help others.

- KINDNESS. Be kind. Just being kind would be a
  gamechanger for a lot of us. Are you kind like Jesus was
  kind?

- HUMILITY. Jesus humbled Himself to the point of death
  for others. Do others see you as a humble man? When is
  the last time you died to self for someone else?

27

- MEEKNESS AND PATIENCE. Authentic men put others first and are even willing to wait on them. Would others describe you as an appropriately meek and patient man?

- FORGIVENESS FOR EACH OTHER. We forgive others just as we have been forgiven. Unearned forgiveness. Who can you give new life to by giving them the unearned gift of forgiveness?

- THE PEACE OF CHRIST RULING IN YOUR HEART. Allow His peace to rule in your heart. Not to just be present . . . but to RULE . . . to take over . . . to consume! For me, I experience this most when I'm creating time and space to be with Jesus, to seek Him. Sometimes in scripture, sometimes in prayer, sometimes in silence. It's then I can feel like I'm breathing in His peace and breathing out my anxieties. Are you setting aside time, inviting His peace to rule in your heart?

- THANKFULNESS. We can choose to focus on everything wrong with everything and everybody, or we can choose to see and be thankful for all of the good and all of our blessings. Being thankful changes how you see. Being thankful changes everything. Do you have a thankful spirit?

— ACTION STEP —

Record in your journal how Paul's encouragement can help shape how you respond to the different challenges in your life.

Who would others say you are? Who do you want to be?

THE CARETAKER

Do you ever find yourself micromanaging everything important in your life? Stress is piling up and life feels out of control, so you become obsessed with regaining and maintaining control? You're constantly trying to rein everything in? It's easy to become obsessed in controlling the things we can as a salve for the things we can't. Because, for some of us, the more we do this, the less we have to feel our anxieties. We just stay busy controlling the things and the people around us so we don't have to confront our inner voids. These voids are trying to tell us something important about ourselves.

If this obsessive control becomes our way of life, we become like a caretaker who always needs to be in control and needed by others. He benefits emotionally from excessively helping and directing others in ways that deprive them of living out their own lives and making their own decisions. Ironically, he often sees himself as honorable, upright, and in charge while his family and close friends see him as overbearing, stifling, or limiting.

The more he micromanages in order to bolster his own self-esteem, the more he robs the self-esteem from those around him.

True caring is about sharing, not about overbearing.

This caretaker persona has a deeply rooted fear that he is not "enough." He feels inadequate and unworthy deep within his soul. In order to mask his fear of deficiency, he becomes an expert "manager." Not only does the "busyness" of this endeavor keep him from feeling his emotional fear and emptiness, he actually convinces himself that he is a worthwhile husband, lover, protector, and father by wearing his caretaker's cloak.

If you find yourself driven by an obsession to control, it's probably an indication that you need to face your inner voids. That you need to courageously delve into your heart and find out the true reason that you feel you don't measure up.

Is it from the wound of an overbearing parent who micromanaged you growing up? Is it from growing up in an explosive home full of conflict? An anxiety-filled home? Maybe you were neglected as a child? It can be difficult and unpleasant to reflect back on our childhoods to answer these kinds of questions. But it is so important for you to do so if you find yourself being an obsessive controller. It's important work to do if you desire to NOT have to control everything, so you can love and empower those around you.

— ACTION STEP —

Be honest with yourself about how others experience you. Answer the preceding questions about your childhood to help you see yourself more clearly.

Do I tend to overmanage my relationships? Do I often feel that I need to control everything in order to measure up? Which wounds from my past are influencing my obsession with control?

THE RUNNER

When we feel insecure inside and haven't done any work toward our emotional maturity, we usually react in one of two ways. We can distract ourself by MICROMANAGING everything, or we can do the opposite: we can fear emotional intimacy so much that we RUN and hide. All we desire is space to breathe and "survive."

We become an avoidant man constantly feeling like we're drowning in a sea of too much intimacy. We find it hard to connect on a deep, emotional level with others. When someone gets a bit too close, we panic and retreat into solitude, addictions, or other distractions. Although hungry for affection and closeness, we inflict upon ourselves the ultimate punishment—total isolation.

We run away. Fast.

For the avoidant man, it can feel like people are always wanting more of us. Once our fear is triggered, we will do anything to create distance, even if it threatens the relationship. This is in reaction to our insecurity and emotional immaturity.

While the avoidant man may crave emotional intimacy, he ends up running from it at all costs. He banishes himself to a desert-like existence, a mere survival, so that he can feel emotionally "safe."

The only way to engage authentically in a real and lasting relationship is to stop running. Stop running and face your fear of

31

intimacy that's keeping you from the fulfilling and satisfying life you truly desire.

— ACTION STEP —

Reflect today on whether you are "running" from important people in your life. Listen to that still, small voice inside that is prompting you to move toward someone important in your life. Pray for the courage to do it in love and humility.

How do I react when someone wants to grow close to me? What kinds of fears drive my reactions? How can I begin to mature in the way I respond to those close to me?

THE ACHIEVEMENT FIX

Addictions come in all shapes and sizes. For many men, it's easy to become addicted to achievement. When we find ourselves taking out our measuring stick or scorecard, applying it to everything we do and comparing it with everybody else, it will never be enough. No matter what we do, we will never measure up. And it usually results in us feeling anxious, worried, deficient, and maybe even depressed.

This drive for achievement often comes from the desire to please someone in our life who historically has been difficult or impossible to please. Oftentimes, it's our dad. We never seem to fully please him or live up to his expectations. When a boy internalizes the message that he doesn't measure up, that little voice goes with him into his manhood. He grows into a man who embodies that inner, critical voice and continues to strive for significance from never-ending achievements and successes. He worries more about what other people think about him than being the man God made him to be.

I love the apostle Paul's prayer in Ephesians 3. He prays that as Christ-followers, we will know the love of God in our inner being . . . in our heart and soul. That we'll know it deeply. That we'll know it in a way that exceeds all other knowledge. That we'll know it in a way that replaces our anxieties and our idol of significance.

An authentic man learns that his security, identity, validation, and well-being don't come from his achievements or outside sources. They come from knowing the love of God in your heart and soul. Knowing it so deeply that it exceeds other knowledge. Knowing it so deeply that it brings a peace and a contentment far greater than any list of achievements you set out to accomplish.

— ACTION STEP —

Pray that you may experience God's love. Allow yourself to receive it.

Am I addicted to achieving for the purpose of impressing others? Do I push myself to achieve because I believe it will make me more worthy of love? Can I allow myself to receive the love of God that takes me even beyond my knowledge about Him?

THE MASKED MAN

Every boy dreams of being a superhero. Growing up, most of us had our favorites. Spiderman, Batman, Iron Man, to name a few. Who were yours? As young boys, these are some of our biggest heroes, they exude everything we learned about masculinity. We wanted to emulate them. We wanted to be them. But did you ever notice, most of them wear masks?

In a sense, this small detail gives us a very big clue as to how we imagine men should be. We remain masked.

We give out as little information about ourselves as possible. Instead, we put forward our hero version, the one we imagine has no faults, flaws, quirks, or baggage.

Why are we so uncomfortable with letting people see who we really are?

For many men, unveiling ourselves emotionally and personally feels threatening and frightening. We fear rejection down to our bones. We imagine that without the mask, we will be just another ordinary guy, or maybe even worse than that.

Here's some great news! God never made anything ordinary. Every person God has ever made is extraordinary in their own unique way, each with his or her own gifts, skills, personality, and characteristics. God tells us that we are all created in His image and are loved by Him, each one of us beautifully unique.

It's amazing what can happen when we remove our masks, having the courage to be transparent with each other. It's truly one of the most freeing things we can do in life. And when we do that, most of the time it frees the other guys around us to do the same. That's when we discover that we're all in this together. We're all dealing with the same stuff . . . the same temptations and failures and embarrassments. There's great power and freedom in removing your mask.

— ACTION STEP —

Prove to yourself that you have the courage to remove your mask. Share what's going on in your life with your close friends. Experience the power and freedom that come with being real.

What masks do I wear at my workplace, in my home, in front of my friends? Why do I fear being seen? What good could happen if I revealed who I truly am to those who love me the most?

THE AUTHENTIC MAN

Everyone hears about Adam, the guy who messed up and trusted the sly serpent instead of God. But have you heard of Adam Number Two? Jesus is the second Adam, the one God sent to get it right where the first Adam got it wrong (1 Corinthians 15:45). It's the second Adam that we follow. He's the one who shows us how to be a real, authentic man.

Sometimes we talk about Adam like we talk about Humpty Dumpty. He had a great fall and then he couldn't be put back together again. The End. But that's not the story of scripture. Instead, God spends years picking up the pieces and trying to mend the relationship between Himself and His creation. Then, He decides to show up on the scene in the form of a human being, His son, Jesus.

Jesus understands what it feels like to be human—the struggles, the pain, the challenges, the temptations. And, in the midst of knowing those things first-hand, He helps us understand how to be the people God intended us to be.

God designed men for a purpose, and Jesus sets the prime example for all of us to follow as men pursuing authentic manhood.

As we observe His life, we see that Jesus puts His Father first. He accepts and loves all people. He puts together a group of drastically different personalities and teaches them to work together as a team. He faces temptation head on and sticks to His mission. He's gentle with those who need love and understanding and firm with those who would stand in God's way. He's strong and He's tender. He's assertive, yet He's caring. He's willing to sacrifice His own life. He demonstrates a servant's heart. He's a life-giving spirit to others. He doesn't hide. He doesn't run. He doesn't fight. He doesn't attack. He stands firm in His beliefs and knows His purpose and nothing will stop Him from living it out.

Learn from Jesus how to live your best, most authentic life. Know His ways. Listen to His wisdom. Know His promises. Everything we need to know about Him can be found in the witnesses to His life that we call the holy scriptures. Jesus is both our inspiration and our model of authentic manhood.

— ACTION STEP —

Get to know Jesus. If you already know Him, get to know Him better. Spend time with Him. You can never know Him well enough. A great way to know more is to read and meditate on the different accounts of His life found in the writings of Matthew, Mark, Luke, and John.

Do I have a personal and intimate relationship with Jesus? What does Jesus truly mean to me in my life? How can I grow as a man by spending time with Jesus and meditating on the testaments to His life in scripture?

SEEK AND FIND

Do you ever feel that your life is idling by? Or that you are moving along but going nowhere? Do you ever just feel empty and lacking hope in anything that really matters?

Many men find themselves feeling these things. We go through the motions of job, family, and community responsibilities but feel no passion or motivation, no joy or investment. We move along, pay the bills, take a vacation, have some hobbies, hang out with friends, but never really feel much meaningful purpose in life —something bigger, deeper, hopeful, eternal.

Maybe you're in a marriage that feels stalled or troubled. Maybe you're in a job that has lost its allure. Or maybe you feel trapped in a dead-end cycle of empty doing and achieving.

Whatever your situation, Jesus has an invitation for you. He invites you to walk through all of your situations with Him. He says that He is the door you can enter to find green pasture (John 10:9-10). His way is the way to the bigger, deeper, hopeful, and eternal things in life. This was part of His purpose in coming to earth. He says He came to earth that we may be saved and that we may have life and have it abundantly. Those are His words. Did you know that? Have you forgotten that? Do you believe that? Have you gone to Him for that?

39

And He also makes a beautiful promise to you. He says that if you seek Him, you will find Him . . . that He will be there for you . . . that even in the midst of the hard and challenging times and all of the emptiness you feel, He has good things for you (Matthew 7:7-11). Maybe even bigger, deeper, hopeful, and eternal things.

If you're facing challenges or feeling empty or lacking hope, maybe a good first step is to admit that the life you are living now isn't the one you want to live. Admit that maybe you can't change things on your own. Remember Jesus' invitation for you to enter His door and walk with Him. Remember His promise to be there for you when you seek Him. This is the path to authentic manhood.

— ACTION STEP —

Set aside time to meditate on the words of Jesus in these passages, both His invitation and His promise to you. Write down some things you would like to invite Him to walk with you in.

Am I taking Jesus up on His offer—that if I seek Him I will find Him?

DEEP INTIMACY

Let's face it. The mention of "deep intimacy" makes a lot of men want to run and hide. Whether due to bravado, saving face, or fear of not measuring up, it's much more comfortable to keep things simple and on the surface. We don't want "heavy" conversation or probing questions. We prefer to keep our deepest feelings deeply and safely tucked away so we don't have to reveal our innermost fears, insecurities, vulnerabilities, or sensitivities. Those kinds of revelations feel threatening to us, and frightening. We fear rejection. We fear facing some things about ourselves that we dislike or feel shame about. But if we refuse to be seen and known, we rob ourselves of the opportunity for deep bonding, true connection, and being fully and wholly loved.

Deep intimacy means that we encounter another person in a truly authentic way. We let all of our faults, our quirks, and every aspect of our personality show. It's the Big Reveal. Engaging in deep intimacy for many men is like shining a light into a long-forgotten cave, whose walls and contents have remained hidden away in the dark for a long, long time. That light will reveal things about us that we have forgotten or haven't ever realized about ourselves. We may be surprised to learn that we feel things that have long been hidden away. That our age-old fears are still lurking there beneath the surface. And this is what is so important to know . . . bringing those hidden things into the light reduces their power over us.

Like "monsters under the bed," when our deepest fears and memories stay hidden, they can feel threatening to us. They can undermine us. But when we reveal them and unmask them, suddenly they don't seem so frightening any longer, and their power has been diminished.

Engaging in deep intimacy feels like a great risk, but it's also an amazing opportunity to be authentically seen and known. It also helps set the stage for us to encourage each other and build each other up as we're encouraged to do in 1 Thessalonians 5:11. Open yourself up so those who love you can encourage you where you need it most. Then you can do the same for them.

Deep intimacy leads to bonding, to deep loving, and to mutual appreciation and respect. The relief, the joy, the fulfillment, and the satisfaction that deep intimacy provides by far outweigh the risk. To know that you are loved and accepted for exactly who you are is the greatest gift any man could hope for.

— ACTION STEP —

Identify the very first thing you see when you shine a flashlight into the depths of your soul. Who do you need to share that with? Share it and enjoy the freedom that goes with bringing it into the light.

What "monsters" of fear and guilt and shame lurk below the surface of the exterior face that I show to the world? How can I begin to trust enough to reveal those parts of myself that I'm ashamed of, that I dislike, or that I have not wanted to face?

Day Twenty-Two

POSITIVITY RESONANCE

Scripture makes it clear from the very beginning, all the way back in Genesis, that we are designed for close relationships. Psychologists describe what all great close relationships have in common as "positivity resonance." You have positivity resonance when you share positive emotions together, demonstrate mutual care toward one another, and behave in sync with one another, emotionally, physically, and spiritually. The more positivity resonance you have with people you are close to, the stronger you are in your relationships.

This doesn't mean you are happy all the time. Every close relationship faces difficulties. But those with positivity resonance keep their positive connection even when the conversation may be tense, difficult, or angry. They never doubt their commitment to one another or their respect for one another, even if times are tough. They love each other.

This is consistent with how scripture talks about love. "Love is patient and kind. . . . It is not arrogant or rude. It does not insist on its own way; it is not irritable or resentful. . . . Love bears all things, believes all things, hopes all things, endures all things" (1 Corinthians 13:4-7).

Whether it's in your marriage, a friendship, or your relationship with God, this kind of resonance makes a relationship vibrant and fosters joy. When people are in tandem with each other and with God, their lives feel more joyful, peaceful, purposeful, and passionate.

Creating this kind of love takes practice and intention. A relationship that develops this kind of love and resonance does so through many small moments and shared experiences.

As you go about your day today, be sure that you are cultivating opportunities to share important moments, to create meaningful shared experiences, and to make time for the special people in your life. Do your part to get to know them on a deep, intimate level, and let them know you care for them by your words and your actions.

— ACTION STEP —

Identify three people in your life you desire to have more positivity resonance with. Identify the attributes from 1 Corinthians 13 that you can grow in the most to deepen those relationships.

Am I giving enough time to cultivate a deep connection in my heart with God? What can I do to initiate moments of "positivity resonance" in my close relationships?

THE MASTER ARCHITECT

Sometimes when things go wrong, it can feel like our world is breaking apart. In those times, we can feel unsure of who we are and what we've built our lives on. Things may not be going the way you expected. Perhaps you've failed in some of your goals, or you've come up empty when you needed to be there for someone. Perhaps you've experienced a failed relationship or a job that didn't work out. When this happens, it's easy to get discouraged and question your own worth, direction, or choices, or even your character. It's one of the main reasons that we need someone in our lives who knows us intimately, who can offer stability, wisdom, and direction, and who can remind us of who we are.

Jesus desires to be that for us. He invites us to come to Him and learn from Him. He assures us that He is gentle and lowly in heart and that, in Him, we can find rest for our souls (Matthew 11:29). Not only has Jesus undergone the ultimate sacrifice for us, He wants to continue being there for us. We can learn from Him and have rest in Him. He shows us in His life how to build upon a solid foundation of faith and how to live a hopeful and meaningful life. He reminds us that we have been created in God's purpose and that we are loved by Him, even when we fail.

In Jesus' lifetime, He was known as a *tekton*, a Greek word meaning "an artisan, craftsman, builder, or architect." The word could also refer to a master of any art. Jesus was master of the art of being human. He understood mistakes. He understood getting things wrong. He understood temptations. He understood disappointment, hurt, and pain. He even understood being let down by other people. By the time he was on the cross, some of His disciples had deserted Him for fear of discovery. And yet He carried on because He knew His purpose.

Invite Jesus in. Let Him support you in all things. He knows who you are. He knows all of your gifts and your skills and your failures and shortcomings. He knows everything you need as a broken and imperfect man.

Sometimes we can get caught up in a kind of perfectionism. We expect ourselves to get everything right the first time. We put pressure on ourselves never to fail. When we do, it's easy to beat ourselves up.

In those times, Jesus reminds us that He's there for us. He invites us to come to Him to find rest.

— ACTION STEP —

Spend some time with Jesus today. Reflect on Matthew 11:29. Share some of your failures and mistakes and disappointments and temptations with Him. Experience His gentleness toward you. Experience His love. Experience His rest.

Have I ever felt like I've failed and my life is falling apart? Can I allow myself to believe that Jesus wants to be there for me in those hard times? Can I receive His invitation to come to Him as He is gentle and lowly and wants to give me rest?

THE ALLURE OF THE EASY CHAIR

You have been given the potential to make a difference in this world. To do that, you've got to be willing to step up when the opportunity arises. Accepting responsibility is one of the things that separates a man from a boy. An authentic man looks for opportunities to serve others and to be a part of solving some of the problems we have in our world.

It's so easy to get sidetracked by our own selfish desires and not even have this on our radar. We put difference-making opportunities on the back burner and focus mainly on our own comfort.

Sometimes we can just be lazy when choosing between serving others or relaxing in the easy chair. The easy chair can seem the easy way out.

We can also become so busy and fill our lives with such constant activities that we never have the time or energy to pursue other initiatives. Or we become so immersed in our own personal entertainment that we're oblivious to opportunities to serve others.

Don't get me wrong, I love my easy chair and am thankful for the respite it gives me at the end of a busy day. And there's certainly nothing wrong with busyness and enjoying personal entertainment. But we weren't designed to live there all the time.

Jesus set a pretty clear example for us in his thirty-three years on earth. He was always moving to where the need was, meeting people in their pain and loss and sickness and confusion. He was always serving and loving others.

You as a man have gifts and skills that you can use not just to pursue your own pleasure and advancement but to better the lives of those around you, to make lasting change in the world, maybe even leading innovative and life-changing initiatives. Discovering your unique skills and gifts and how you can apply them to help others is part of your journey to authentic manhood. It's part of how you become a life-giving spirit in the lives of others.

There is nothing you can do in this life that will give you more meaning and more joy than when you do something to serve and bless and help others.

— ACTION STEP —

Spend some time thinking and praying today about some ways you can use your gifts and abilities to bless and serve somebody else.

How can I use the gifts that God has given me to make a difference in the world? Can I commit today to reject passivity in my life and to engage with the world in ways that make a difference?

FIGHTING DRAGONS

Did you ever fantasize about fighting the evil dragons when you were a kid? We've all dreamed of being the hero, of being the warrior who can defeat the enemy. You probably never had to stare down a fire-breathing dragon, but as you've grown up and entered adulthood, you realized at some point that dragons are real. They're not the fire-breathing kind, but they can pose a formidable threat to our intentions in life—I'm talking about the dragons of insecurity, anxiety, guilt, and shame. These dragons can incinerate our courage and sap our spirit the instant we begin to feel some victories in life. We may appear to be armored wonders in our face to the world, brave and true. But inside, our hearts are burning with shame and melting with fear that some-one will discover the "weakness" we feel inside, that someone will discover we're really not heroes at all. That sometimes, we're even cowering failures.

This feeling that we are "not good enough" or "not brave enough" can keep us so busy battling our inner soul-eaters that it saps our energy for doing nearly anything else. When our inner dragons rear their heads, we can become distracted, descend into our caves, and begin to fail in our responsibilities and relation-ships, even the ones that mean so much to us. It takes more and

49

more energy for us to keep up our armored façade. Soon, we begin to feel burned out, burned up, and utterly exhausted.

Why does this happen? We become so busy fighting our invisible dragons that we have no time or fuel to fight the real threats coming our way.

How can we slay our dragons of insecurity and shame? The only way is to face them head on, to bring them out of the cave and into the light, where they will be revealed for the posers they truly are. Once dragged into the light, they lose their fire and flame. Our insecurities and our shame cannot survive when we allow ourselves to see them and own them and talk about them.

Your dragons are not who you are. Don't let them rule you but slay them by revealing them as strength-sapping figments. When you do this you become like a warrior who is defeating the enemy. Scripture tells you that you are a man made in God's image. When you embrace your God-given, authentic identity, you walk in a new freedom to love and be loved and to slay the dragons of insecurity, anxiety, guilt, and shame.

— ACTION STEP —

Write down things that are making you feel anxious and insecure. Writing them down, seeing them, and owning them is often the first step toward defeating them and moving past them. Share them with someone close and invite Jesus to walk with you in them.

Do I have a healthy awareness of my own inner dragons? What steps can I take to own them, bring them into the light, and slay them so I can enjoy the freedom to be who God made me to be?

Day Twenty-Six

MY TEAM

In order for us to lead courageously in life, every one of us needs a team of other men, a circle of close friends, in which we can share our experiences, stories, challenges, wins, and failures. We need to know that we have others in our corner, to walk with us, to encourage us, to keep us accountable to our goals in life, and to fight with us for causes that matter.

A man who has teammates knows his fellow brothers will stand up for him and stand by him, even when he makes mistakes. He knows they will never reject him because he is a valued member of their team. His faithful brothers provide a circle of friends who will be loyal to the end and honest to a fault. Within this group, he can be entirely himself and can find the support and encouragement he needs to mature and grow into the man he wants to become.

Jesus knew the benefit and power of a circle of loyal men. He spent three years building loyalty and unity among them despite differences in their experiences, personalities, origins, and views. He taught them how to be a team. He knew they would need each other in the challenges ahead. They were able to lead courageously in the ways they did because of their bond together and their shared mission with Him.

If you do not have a team of trusted and valued men in your life to help you travel this road toward authentic manhood, start working on that today. Make it a high priority. Doing life together with others is always better than alone and by yourself.

— ACTION STEP —

Make a list of the guys who are on your team. The guys you can go to with anything, who have your back no matter what, who make you better than you would be by yourself, and who encourage you and build you up. Know who they are.

Do I have trusted friends in my life to whom I can turn no matter what happens and with whom I can share my darkest secrets and biggest challenges? If not, who should I invite to be on my team? If so, what remains hidden and unshared with them?

INVESTING FOR THE LONG HAUL

All investments, whether they be financial, spiritual, emotional, or career-related, carry a degree of risk. The primary question for any man choosing to invest will always be about what he could gain and what he could lose. In order to maximize most investments, you must be willing to commit to it for the "long haul."

Almost every investment will experience ups and downs, wins and losses along the way. Only when you're in it for the duration can you truly expect a positive return. Whether it's a battle, a journey, a project, or an emotional or relational investment, the process remains the same. You need to be willing to go the distance.

Emotional investments can feel especially risky, especially when the outcomes don't seem clear. But a true investor knows that the greater and deeper the investment, the more likely the outcome will be positive over the long haul. Relationships develop over time. They improve with increasing degrees of emotional and spiritual investment. They become dependent upon how much and how long you are willing to commit.

Think about the investments in your life. Do you commit to your projects or relationships with reticence? With conditions? Within a limited timeframe? With only "one foot in" in order to protect yourself from being hurt? The irony is that only those willing to invest broadly and deeply and for the long haul will reap the true rewards and the satisfaction of growing something meaningful and fulfilling.

Scripture calls us to "love each other *deeply*" (1 Peter 4:8, NIV, emphasis added). That means below the surface. That means even when things get tough. That means with all of your heart. Whether in your relationship with your work, your wife, your children, or God, it's how much you are willing to risk your heart over the long haul that will determine how your forever will play out and pay out.

— ACTION STEP —

Take some time today to reflect on the emotional and spiritual investments you are making in your relationships.

Have I been too risk-averse in my most important relationships? Has my inability to commit deeply affected my relationships? Will my life improve and become deeper and more meaningful if I take greater risks and invest more deeply over the long haul?

IDENTITY

We all have an identity. The dictionary defines *identity* as "the condition of being oneself, and not another . . . the character as to who a person is; the qualities, beliefs, etc., that distinguish or identify a person."

What's *your* identity? How would you answer that? How would your family and friends answer that?

We begin being told what our identity should be early on in life. It usually begins with our parents or primary caregivers. Then it expands over time to our extended family, our teachers, coaches, friends, pastors, co-workers, bosses. It grows even more from the books we read, the movies we watch, the social media streams we're on, the influencers we follow, etc. Some of the messaging is loud and clear and a lot of it is subtle and indirect. We get all kinds of mixed signals about what our identity should be as a man. A lot of the information seems to revolve around what I call THE BIG THREE:

1. What we should DO (e.g., job, career, sports, hobbies, travel, get married, stay single, etc.);

2. What we should HAVE (e.g., cars, homes, money, clothes, good looks, wisdom, common sense, humor, etc.); and

3. What we want OTHERS TO THINK about us (e.g., smart, leader, cool, kind, tough, wealthy, spiritual, funny, etc.).

Having been told these things all of our lives, it's easy to let them shape our identity primarily around worldly things . . . that is, "the flesh."

The apostle Paul gives us some helpful wisdom as we reflect on our identities. There was a time in Paul's life when THE BIG THREE dominated his own identity. He said he had more reason to be "confident in the flesh" than anyone (Philippians 3:4). He had quite the impressive resume. He was born into the right family, he was a member of the right tribe, a loyal keeper of the law, an acknowledged top leader in the hierarchy, a zealous persecutor of the opposition, and he was blameless for his pristine track record . . . that is, until he was blinded by the light and knocked off his horse . . . and God grabbed his heart . . . and he received a new vision for his life.

He discovered a new identity, an identity that gave him new hope in both life and death. It even gave him a new citizenship. He says in Philippians 3:8-9 that once God grabbed his heart and he was introduced to the love and grace of Jesus, he "count[ed] everything [else] as loss because of the surpassing worth of knowing Christ Jesus my Lord. For his sake I have suffered the loss of all things and count them as rubbish, in order that I may gain Christ and be found in him, not having a righteousness of my own . . . but that which comes through faith in Christ." In a different letter, Paul identifies himself not as the man who has it all, but as an apostle of Christ Jesus, having been adopted by him as a son (Ephesians 1).

Paul encourages us, as we consider our own identity, to imitate him . . . to seek our identity in something bigger and deeper than just what we DO, what we HAVE, and what OTHERS THINK about us. He encourages us to find our ultimate identity as adopted sons of Christ, in His love and in His grace.

— ACTION STEP —

Write in your journal the important things that make up your identity. Take some time to reflect on that.

Which of THE BIG THREE do you identify with the most? Do you identify as the man striving to have it all or as a man counting everything as loss because of the worth of knowing Christ Jesus?

TRUST AND DO GOOD

Psalm 37:3-4 is one of my favorite Psalms. In it, King David offers some really simple, but profound, encouragement as we're reflecting on who we are and how we're designed. It simply says:

> Trust in the LORD, and do good;
>
>> dwell in the land and befriend faithfulness.
>
> Delight yourself in the LORD,
>
>> and he will give you the desires of your heart.

Trust in the Lord. What does it look like and feel like when you're truly placing your trust in the Lord and not yourself or your circumstances or your job or your bank account or your hobbies, etc.? Are you truly letting go and seeking Him and His will and His way?

Do good. Pretty simple. Do good things. Do good for others. Do good for your family. Do good in your work. Do good for your enemies (yep). Do good. What does it look like when you're focused on doing good in your life?

Befriend faithfulness. I like that. Make faithfulness your friend. You know, faithfulness can include doubts and questions. It doesn't say make "certainty" your friend. It says faithfulness. What does it look like when you're friends with faithfulness?

Delight yourself in the Lord. Hopefully, reading that makes your heart smile. To me, that means being deeply encouraged and overwhelmed by God's goodness, His love, His grace, His presence, His will, His interest in hearing my prayer. It means . . . being all-in with Him in all things. How do you delight in the Lord?

And he will give you the desires of your heart. Ahh, what a promise! A big promise! But I personally don't think "desires of our heart" means our Christmas wish list. I think it means God knows the deepest desires of our heart . . . to be fully loved and accepted. And when we're trusting Him and doing good and being faithful and delighting in His goodness, we can personally experience that love and acceptance. From Him. From others. And we can feel like we matter in this world and that we have a purpose and a place and a God who knows us and cares about us.

— ACTION STEP —

Write in your journal what it looks like for you to live out this passage.

How does this scripture speak to you?

MISSING THE MARK

We all miss our mark at times. Whether we're throwing darts, shooting a basketball, trying to reach a new goal, or just living life, we all miss sometimes—even those who practice the most and take it the most seriously. But the more important thing is that we have a mark. A target that we're aiming for and shooting at. And in life itself, it's most important to have targets that matter. Targets that make us who we are. Targets that shape our direction and determine where we end up. Targets that shape the meaning of our lives.

Jesus' disciples asked Him one day what they should be aiming at. They asked Him which of the commandments were most important. They wanted to know which ones should be their main targets.

Jesus didn't hesitate in His response. He said the most important ones were the ones about love, the ones calling us to love God and love people. He said those two commandments sum up all the others. And then He lived them out by example.

He went to where people were hurting and sick. He followed His Father's will unto death . . . a death that He died for others. His main targets in life were clearly to love God the Father and to love and care about people. Jesus gave us a pretty simple and clear target for our lives.

— ACTION STEP —

Identify the main things you're aiming for in life. Ask those closest to you what it seems to them that you're aiming for. Listen with an open mind for what you might need to hear from them.

What are you aiming for in your life as a man? What does it look like for you to love God and love people like Jesus?

Day Thirty-One

DIAMOND IN THE ROUGH

The phrase "diamond in the rough" derives from diamonds that, found in nature, can be rough and uneven with no apparent value. But, when they are cut and polished, their multiple facets are revealed and they glisten with beauty. They become beautiful and valuable.

The most common diamond has 58 facets. Some have 64. Larger diamonds can have as many as 144 facets. These multiple "faces" allow for the diamond to fulfill its full potential as a premium, sought-after gem. Although diamonds come in different shapes and sizes, their prism-like quality contributes to their appeal.

We men can be like a "diamond in the rough." We may have the potential to bring exceptional leadership and dependable stability to our homes, workplaces, and communities, but we sometimes need first to define, refine, and hone the various "faces" of our masculinity. We have the potential to shine through each of our different "faces," but may find it challenging to transition well from one to another.

Can you be the humble, take-charge leader you need to be at work but come home and be the compassionate listener and empathetic friend you need to be for your family? Can you be the courageous knight who fights for injustice in the world but then extend a hand of peace to those who differ in opinion on what to make for dinner? Can you, like Jesus, be both a world-changer and a lover? Can you transition from one to the other as though turning a diamond in the light? Are you the same person no matter where you are or who you're with, but allowing different facets of your personality to shine the brightest in one moment or another?

It's important to be aware that while we want to be the same authentic man wherever we are, in whatever we're doing, and whoever we're with, we do have different "faces" of our personality to offer in different settings. It's helpful to know the different "faces" you have to offer and to be aware as you transition from one to another in order to best fit the setting and the need. Knowing your true self and living authentically helps you live out your different "faces" in ways that bless those around you.

— ACTION STEP —

Be honest with yourself and identify the different "faces" you have to offer others. Being aware of the different "faces" you have to offer is helpful as you consider ways to serve others.

Do I ever put on my work-face when I'm at home with my family? How can I better embrace all of the roles in my life while remaining rooted and secure in my core identity?

Day Thirty-Two

HIDDEN AND ISOLATED

Do you ever share your deepest secrets or darkest fears with your closest friends? What about sharing your regrets or feelings or worries or inadequacies or mistakes or sins? It's not a question of whether we have any of these things in our lives. We all do. It's part of being human. The question is . . . what do you do with these things? Do you try to hide them for "self protection"?

Sometimes we feel afraid to share our feelings of stress and inadequacy, especially with our friends. When we get together, it's easy to talk about sports, our intellectual pursuits, our jobs, or our families, but usually on a mostly superficial level. We worry that if we share our true feelings and emotions, we'll "lose face" with our friends as an "able and successful" guy. Even if we feel like we're dying inside, when our buddies ask us how we're doing, we usually will answer, "Everything is fine!" It can feel hard to let down that "tough-guy, have-it-all-together" façade.

When we hide and bury our worries and our fears, we become spiritually isolated and alone in our pain. When we don't have a safe place to share these things, they fester and almost always come out in less-than-helpful ways.

Men were not meant to be loners. This is not your true face and you're not showing your true face.

65

We weren't designed to live hidden and isolated lives. We are emotional and spiritual beings made to live in healthy, authentic community with others. Scripture reminds us we need that for the health of our souls.

Walk in the light and have fellowship with one another (1 John 1:7).

Confess our sins to one another that we may be healed (James 5:16).

As iron sharpens iron, one man sharpens another (Proverbs 27:17).

Yes, it takes courage to allow your feelings and problems to surface in an intentional way, to reveal your true self to your trusted friends and family. But when we do step into that courage and get things out in the light, we experience new strength and a freedom that leads us toward healing instead of hiding.

— ACTION STEP —

Identify a couple of your deepest worries and greatest fears in life. Take the step of courage needed to share them with people you trust. More than likely, it will give them permission to do the same with you.

Are you hiding? Do you feel spiritually isolated? What secret or fear could you share with a trusted friend that would give you a new freedom and help you step toward healing? Who can you share that with?

THE QUEST FOR THE HOLY GRAIL

Stories of the search for the elusive "holy grail"—the communion cup of Christ—permeated Medieval literature in many different languages. You may remember that Monty Python even created their own comedic version of the quest for the grail and its purported healing power, eternal youth, and everlasting happiness, satirizing the myth with their "unholy" antics. But the fantasy to "age backwards," to find the secret elixir to happiness, to leave responsibilities behind, and to embrace endless boyish pursuits is all too real for many men.

Life can be stressful, overwhelming, and just hard at times. When it is, it's easy to get lost in a great nostalgia for our boyhood days of pleasure, games, and leisure. While fond memories can be entertaining or comforting, if we don't have a grown-up vision we're moving toward, it's easy to fall back into adolescent-style escapes and enter into an illusory and dangerous "myth" of our own making. A myth that will never lead us to a life of meaning, passion, and purpose.

Don't spend your life chasing proverbial carrots. When you do, you miss ample and rich opportunities right in front of you that may deeply enrich your life. Sure, true and meaningful goals may feel harder to attain or take more time and energy to achieve, but in the long term, the pursuit of meaningful, spiritually centered goals can bring much more growth, satisfaction, and true fulfillment for every man.

The obsessive quest for an "easy" life can, in fact, lead a man down a dangerous, identity-stealing, joy-robbing, self-esteem–destroying path.

While the path toward authentic manhood may require you to take courageous steps toward building and maintaining relationships, exploring and healing your wounds, and establishing a firm identity in Christ, the joy you reap will by far outweigh the elusive allure of the "grail."

— ACTION STEP —

Write down the meaningful and spiritually centered goals you have for yourself in this season of life. Reflect on the things you are doing to move toward those.

Am I searching for happiness in all the wrong places? Can I make a commitment to some meaningful goals that will help me grow in the areas of life that matter the most?

Day Thirty-Four

HEART, SOUL, MIND, AND STRENGTH

When the "Father of Soul" Ray Charles lost his sight at only seven years old from juvenile glaucoma, his family sent him to the Florida School for the Deaf and Blind. During his eight years at the school, Ray learned how to play multiple instruments, how to read and write music in Braille, and how to navigate the world without the help of his eyes. Ray reached beyond his wildest dreams and achieved his true potential by engaging his head, hands, and heart in his music. He learned a more intimate way to engage with the world that required all of his remaining faculties.

Like most arts, relational intimacy demands this same thing of us. If we only engage in our relationships with our intellects or our brains, we can appear to be emotionally aloof, disengaged, uncaring, or unfeeling. If we only engage with our emotions, we can seem overwhelming, unable to establish appropriate boundaries, or lacking in reason or negotiation skills. If we only engage physically or sexually, we come across as robotic, lacking in sensuality, emotional intimacy, warmth, and sensitivity.

True relational intimacy requires us to embrace all facets of ourselves. Jesus calls us to love with all of our *heart* and *soul* and *mind* and *strength* (Mark 12:30-31). That is the kind of love He desires from us. And He tells us to love each other fully, as we love

69

ourselves. . . . Authentic relationships are holistically connected relationships. The more fully and completely we engage with all of our heart, soul, mind, and strength, the more satisfying and fulfilling ALL of our relationships will feel.

— ACTION STEP —

Spend some time reflecting on how you love with your heart . . . your soul . . . your mind . . . and your strength.

What aspects are missing from my current relationships? In which of these areas do I need to grow the most? What are some simple steps toward that?

A WAY TO LIVE

A large crowd of people gathered to hear Jesus speak one day. This is what He had to say:

> Blessed are those who hunger and thirst for righteousness . . .
> Blessed are the merciful . . .
> Blessed are the pure in heart . . .
> Blessed are the peacemakers . . .
> You are the salt of the earth and the light of the world.

Jesus' words (Matthew 5) echo the words of the prophet Micah (Micah 6:8) when he tells us what the Lord desires from us:

> to do justice . . .
> to love kindness . . .
> to walk humbly with God.

For the man who desires the way of Jesus, there is a way to live. God allows us to decide if we will live that way. We decide if we want to show *mercy* to others, especially when it's to a person who has caused us difficulties. We decide if we desire a *pure heart* and want to *make peace* even when it means giving up something for ourselves. We decide if we're going to be *salt and light* to a hurting and lonely world. We decide if we're going to *love kindness* and *walk humbly* in an oftentimes mean and unfair world.

These are daily if not hourly decisions. It seems to me that these "ways to live" are born out of what Jesus says is the most important thing of all . . . love.

It's tempting to be self-righteous and selfish and out to win at all costs. Jesus says that there are blessings to be received when we live His way. Blessed are ...

— ACTION STEP —

Reflect and meditate on the words of Jesus in this passage. Let them be imprinted in your heart. Let them guide the way you live.

Would others say that this is the way you live?

STRENGTH IN HUMILITY

Sometimes a man can confuse strength of character with strength of control. Bullying and bossiness is not the kind of strength that changes the world. It's true, this world can be a cruel and harsh place. Some days it seems like if we don't fight fire with fire, we will be crushed. It can be tempting to abandon our character and do whatever it takes to win . . . to abandon any notion of a tender heart.

But the way of Christ is a way of humility and tenderness and even gentleness. He lived and led with a heart that even He described as "gentle and lowly" (Matthew 11:29). The apostle Paul referenced Jesus as the ultimate example of humility, reminding us how He took the form of a servant despite being in the form of God and even humbled Himself to the point of death (Philippians 2:5-8).

As authentic men following the way of Jesus, let us set out to be humble in all of our ways. Let us set out to make our strength of character something that is very important to us and that can be trusted by others. Let your strength and empowerment come from your faith, your humility, and your good character, not from unharnessed aggression or mean-spiritedness.

An authentic man does not lash out without thought or purpose and does not destroy others for his selfish goals. He knows that unbridled power is dangerous. He walks in the empowerment of Christ toward being a life-giving spirit to others.

When we make power for our own pleasure the aim, bad things happen. Rather than doing good and serving others, we can become self-absorbed and unrepentant of our harmful, destructive, and controlling deeds.

The way of Jesus is the way of humility, grace, mercy, and love for others.

— ACTION STEP —

Spend some time with Jesus today reflecting on your spirit of humility.

At what times in my life have I used my power selfishly or unjustly? Have I made amends to those I've hurt? What would it mean for me to surrender my personal power and take on the empowerment of Christ? How would doing this change my way of dealing with others?

CRIPPLING DOUBT

Every man has a bit of doubt buried deeply within his psyche. Doubt isn't always a bad thing. It's part of life. If we're honest, we can even own the reality that doubt is part of our faith journey. It's a necessary part of "working out our faith." But if we let it, that inner nugget of doubt can grow and eat away at our faith, cripple our confidence, and even deplete our ability to take initiative when we know we should.

When we're unaware of the presence of our doubt, it can begin to sabotage us from within. We can doubt our ability to make a difference in the world. We can become so fearful and insecure inside that we spend all of our energy doing everything imaginable so others will like us. Have you every experienced that?

If you have, you might have found yourself becoming a yes-man, a people pleaser, unable to establish boundaries in your life for your own benefit and the benefit of others. You may have become afraid that your kids won't like you if you set boundaries so you avoid making important parental decisions. You avoid teaching them responsibility and consequences for their actions. You may have become fearful of angering your wife or girlfriend so you defer all decisions to her and harbor your frustrations inside, fearful of conflict and its resulting consequences.

You fear that if people truly saw who you are inside they surely would be disappointed, so you hide your doubts and fears about yourself and refuse to let anyone see who you really are. You forget that much of your strength and confidence is grown in Christ and that your restoration and renewal are in Him, from the inside out.

Instead of being crippled by our doubts and paralyzed by our insecurities, Jesus invites us to cast all of our anxieties on Him. The apostle Peter, who was an eyewitness to Jesus' life, encourages us to give all of our anxieties and fears to Jesus because He cares for us (1 Peter 5:7) . . . to throw all of our burdens and doubts to Him and let Him carry them for us. We can stop, let go of our doubts and anxieties, and say . . . "Here, Jesus." I like to actually open my hand to Him and say, "Here, I give my doubts and fears to You." I may say it ten times in a day.

Once your ultimate trust lies in Jesus and not in yourself, you can be confident and assured of your worth in Him . . . even in the midst of your doubts.

— ACTION STEP —

Simply close your eyes, go to Jesus, and say "HERE." Open your hand to Him and give Him all of your doubts, your anxieties, and your fears.

Do I hang on to my doubts and allow them to cripple me or do I prayerfully give them to Jesus?

Day Thirty-Eight

SEEING AND HEALING

It takes great courage to look at ourselves with honesty and truth, to be willing to see things in ourselves that may not be easy to see. We all have it . . . the stuff we'd rather just bury than deal with or let others see . . . the hurts and habits and mistakes and wounds from the past. But unless we're willing to see those things and deal with them, they will own us and shape who we are.

It can be difficult for us to see a lot of these dark things on our own. It usually takes someone else who knows us well, cares for us deeply, and is willing to be honest with us to help us see them. And it takes us being willing to listen. Even when it's uncomfortable. Even when we don't want to. Even if it may require change. It's only when we're willing to see ourselves as we really are, the good and the bad, that we can begin to heal and live in freedom.

We all have a story that defines us. All of our stories are filled with both joys and wounds. Yes, every single one of us has wounds. And some of us are blessed to also have scars.

Scars are healed wounds. Healed wounds are much healthier than unhealed wounds. Being able to tell your full story to others and show them your scars is one of the most meaningful and influential things you can do with your life. Your story of healing and redemption can give them a vision for their own healing.

77

But it all begins with us being willing to see . . . to see ourselves as we really are . . . to see and then to be willing to share the hidden things in a safe place . . . to bring them into the light . . . to be open and vulnerable with safe people who care . . . to begin the healing process. Are you ready to move toward healing and freedom or do you want to stay stuck in your wounds?

— ACTION STEP —

Be honest with yourself about your unhealed wounds. Write them down in your journal. If you were your best friend, what encouragement would you give yourself about taking a step toward healing?

Do I have the courage see myself fully, to expose the hidden shadows and begin the process of healing my hurts and wounds?

Day Thirty-Nine

THE SHADOW

Some men hate to admit this, but the fact is we are complex emotional beings. We carry all kinds of memories, experiences, judgments, and images of ourselves and the world around us. From these, we create our story. Our story represents the entirety of our identity—both what we see as the good and what we see as the bad. To accept ourselves as God accepts us, we need to embrace our entire story, not just the good parts.

When we neglect parts of our story and refuse to confront our wounds, we end up spending most of our time living in the shadow of our "true self." We find ourselves living in our "false self." Your "false self" is also your "less-than self." Instead of becoming an authentic man who faces up to your wounds and works toward healing them, you allow those wounds to fester inside of you. This can cause havoc in your life, especially as the wounds bubble to the surface in unhealthy ways.

When you fail to see yourself fully and fail to do the work to heal, you limp through life. You end up becoming someone you don't want to be. You end up hurting your most important relationships and destroying a lot of the good in your life.

You divide yourself into the story you wish to tell and the story you hide within.

The road toward authentic manhood requires you to do the difficult work of confronting, healing, and embracing your own story—both the good parts and those difficult or painful to face.

To do this, you need the support of other trustworthy men, of your family, of your therapist or counselor, and of Jesus . . . the ultimate grace-giver. Confronting what you see as the dark parts of yourself and embracing them as part of who you are, part of your story, takes immense strength, courage, and initiative. It also takes the desire to become the liberated and whole person you were created to be. With God's help and the support of others around you, you can do this.

— ACTION STEP —

Look back at the hurts and wounds you wrote down in your journal yesterday. Take some positive steps today toward healing. Make amends where you need to make amends. Reach out to a counselor if you need help understanding your hurts and wounds more clearly. Share your heart with a friend. They need to be on this journey as much as you do.

What parts of myself cause me shame, pain, or guilt? Do I have the courage to look at my shadow places, acknowledge them, and begin to dispel their power over me by prayerfully giving them to Jesus and sharing them in a safe place?

NO VICTIMS ALLOWED

Life can feel like a constant battle, sometimes a losing one. Maybe life has thrown you some curve balls. Maybe you've battled depression, anxiety, fear, or some sort of addiction. It's easy to become weary from battling each and every day without knowing how to find relief.

Even when you feel defeated, you do have choices. You can choose to make things better by doing what you need to do to rally. Or, you can make things even worse by throwing up your hands and choosing the way of the *victim*, lashing out and blaming everything and everyone around you for your lot in life.

A man who claims victimhood in essence shifts responsibility for the state of his life onto other people and circumstances. Anything bad that happens? He expects it's due to the vendetta life has against him. Instead of nobly fighting for the betterment of himself and others, he keeps himself busy pointing to the forces that make it impossible for him ever to win. When you become the victim, you give yourself permission to sit back and not try. Somewhere inside, the victim believes that he can't lose if he refuses to take responsibility for any of it. That's a defeatist attitude and a victim mentality.

A tendency toward victimhood usually arises from a fragile place within. You may have perfectionist tendencies and find it difficult to accept criticism or failure. You may find it difficult to accept yourself and your weaknesses. A false image of masculinity may have you demanding too much of yourself based on unreasonable expectations. To fail feels like the ultimate emasculation. The victim comes to believe that if you can blame outside forces, maybe your image remains intact.

If you allow yourself to fall into a victim mentality, you will always lack true fulfillment and peace. Because deep inside, you know the truth.

Of all people who've ever lived, Jesus could easily have fallen into a victimhood mentality. He could have blamed everybody who failed Him and mistreated Him. He could have quit on His life quest. Instead, He chose to step into His story and to trust His Father. He was honest with His Father about His fears, but then He trusted Him fully for His purpose.

— ACTION STEP —

Spend some time in Galatians 6:9. Reflect on Paul's encouragement for us to not grow weary in doing good, to not give up . . . and take heart in what he says is likely to happen in due season.

Have I allowed myself to fall into a victim mentality at some point in my life? Do I sometimes fear failure so much that it's easier not to try? Can I follow the way of Jesus, hand my fears over to God, and trust Him for my purpose even when life feels hard and unfair?

THE HEART OF A MAN

In our culture, men are often thought of as having hearts of steel and spines of iron. Strong and able with thick skin, covered in protective armor. Hunters, gatherers, providers, and protectors. While we certainly should be protectors, providers, and leaders, we can also be compassionate, sensitive, sacrificial, and emotional. In fact, a man who embraces an authentic form of masculinity understands himself as all of these.

Tender hearts make us approachable, relational, connective, and romantic. We take time to listen to the voice of others. We pick up on our wife's emotional needs and offer her comfort, encouragement, and support. Our physical affection is accompanied by deep emotional connection.

The tender-hearted and relational man opens up his heart to family and close friends and reveals his joys, fears, and flaws. He doesn't spend time pretending or hiding. He needs no divisions. He desires to connect emotionally and spiritually and feels contentment and joy in responding to the needs of others.

He can be a grizzly one moment when he needs to protect the ones he loves from danger, yet a teddy bear in the next when he wants to comfort and connect with his family and friends.

The way of Jesus is to cultivate a tender heart that loves and cares for other people. Jesus refers to himself as "gentle and lowly in heart." We see Him time after time coming near to people, to meet them where they are and to care about their needs. Offering a tender and caring heart to others is an important part of living out our manhood. A tender heart is one of the true marks of an authentic man.

ACTION STEP

Read Matthew 11:29-30. Reflect on these words of Jesus and pray for the same "gentle and lowly heart" that He offers to us.

Do I connect with my family and close friends at deep and emotional levels? Do other people see me as a tender-hearted man who cares for the needs of other people? How can I better cultivate a tender heart to be more like Jesus?

Day Forty-Two
SKIPPING ROCKS

Have you ever stood on a river bank and killed a little time by just skipping rocks across the water? You look for that perfect rock with a flat side, one that will ride the surface for the longest time.

Some of us think of our relationships much like we do skipping rocks. It's a surface game. Just as the stone barely touches the water, we keep our relationships going on a surface level. We miss the beauty and wonder of true emotional and heart-level connection . . . the kind of connection that we were made for.

In order to go below the surface in our close relationships, we must be willing to explore our own inner world, to know what's going on below our own surface. We need to devote some time, effort, and focus to explore the presence and depths of our feelings and emotions. Many men are hesitant, and even afraid, to go there. We think it makes us feel weak and not strong.

But when we figure out that our feelings and emotions are tools God gives us to understand what's going on below the surface . . . it changes everything. We begin to see that we have the tools we need to connect at a heart level in our closest relationships.

Going below the surface to be honest about and aware of what's in your heart will help you take your close relationships

85

to another level. You'll be better equipped to be truly present, engaged, invested, and committed. It may feel uncomfortable at first, but you will eventually have a hard time staying on the surface in your close relationships because there is so much more meaning and substance and real connection below the surface.

Skimming the surface in your life can give people the impression that you've got everything "together." But you'll always be limiting yourself in terms of your spiritual depth and emotional maturity. God made us in His image to be emotional and spiritual beings and to have deep and meaningful relationships with each other. Jesus models that for us in His relationship with His heavenly Father. He also models it in the intimate community He fosters with His disciples. In our path to authentic manhood, we need authentic relationships where we can go deep.

Leave behind the boyhood temptation to be like a stone skipping along the surface of the water. Deep friendships refresh the soul. Go deep and begin to enjoy the refreshment of heart-level connections with both your Father in heaven and the important people in your life.

— ACTION STEP —

Thank the people who are willing to go deep with you. They are a gift to you.

Am I skipping along the surface of life with no deep and meaningful relationships? Do I allow a little discomfort and fear to keep me from sharing my true heart in my closest relationships?

THE ART OF PAINTING

The apostle Paul tells us to rejoice in our sufferings. We don't like to hear that, but he reminds us that our sufferings can produce endurance. And our endurance produces character, and character produces hope. And our hope is fulfilled as we receive the love of God into our hearts (Romans 5:3-5).

Sometimes our greatest growth occurs during our greatest adversities. The choices we make and the places we look for hope during those times, whether good or bad, will help shape who we are as men.

Every one of our lives is like a painting in progress. Each day, the experiences and challenges we undertake will add new colors, textures, shades, and images to our developing portrait. Our personal portrait will be unique to us—filled with shapes, lines, shades of light and shades of grey, some areas clear and some blurred, even some mistakes. Your life is your canvas, and you have been given, at least in part, the amazing gift of writing your story.

Some days, you may need to cross boundaries or blend colors to create a new image when your brush has deviated off of its intended course. Other days, you may struggle to feel creative at all. And that's okay, it's part of the process.

Suffering . . . endurance . . . character . . . hope . . . love. As you write your story, it's really important to develop the ability to adapt, to take a smudge and from it create new beauty, not to see the honest mistakes in your life as doomed splotches on your character but to learn how to take those mistakes and create from them something new and even beautiful.

To learn the "art of painting" is to learn to forgive yourself, to receive the forgiveness and hope offered in Christ, to do the work toward identifying and healing your wounds, to accept your past as part of who you are, and to create from out of that muddle the masterpiece God designed you to be.

— ACTION STEP —

Identify things that you need to forgive yourself for, just as Christ has forgiven you.

How can my mistakes of the past become opportunities for creating a different future? How can I embrace my pain from the past and use it creatively to build a renewed sense of meaning, passion, and purpose for my life?

Day Forty-Four
BE GRATEFUL

Are you a grateful person? Do you enjoy being around grateful people? Did you know you are designed for gratefulness? Reflect on these words: "Rejoice always, . . . *give thanks in all circumstances*; for this is the will of God in Christ Jesus for you" (1 Thessalonians 5:16-18) (emphasis added).

It's hard to be grateful when life doesn't go our way. But being grateful is a choice. We can choose to be grateful no matter our circumstances.

Here are some things we can let keep us from being grateful: envy, materialism, comparison, cynicism, selfishness, arrogance, narcissism, judging, resentment.

Not only is your gratefulness a gift to those around you, it can also be for your own benefit. Recent studies by the Mayo Clinic show that expressing gratitude is associated with a host of mental and physical benefits. They have shown that being a grateful person can improve your sleep, your mood, and your levels of immunity. Gratitude can even decrease depression, anxiety, chronic pain, and risk of disease.

Being grateful is a good thing for a lot of reasons. It's a consistent theme emphasized throughout scripture:

> "Give thanks always and for everything to God the Father in the name of our Lord Jesus Christ" (Ephesians 5:20).

89

"Do not be anxious about anything, but in everything by prayer and supplication with thanksgiving let your requests be made known to God" (Philippians 4:6).

"This is the day that the LORD has made; let us rejoice and be glad in it" (Psalms 118:24)

"And let the peace of Christ rule in your hearts, to which indeed you were called in one body. And be thankful" (Colossians 3:15).

"Oh give thanks to the LORD, for he is good, for his steadfast love endures forever" (Psalms 107:1).

"Count it all joy, my brothers, when you meet trials of various kinds, for you know that the testing of your faith produces steadfastness" (James 1:2-3).

— ACTION STEP —

Take time to reflect on these passages. Be reminded and encouraged that God designed you to be a grateful man.

Are you a grateful person? What are the circumstances that sometimes keep you from having a grateful spirit? Do you try to look for the good in other people and in your circumstances?

THE NEED FOR CONNECTION

Men, every single one of us craves connection and emotional intimacy. It doesn't matter if you're an introvert, extrovert, or ambivert. We all want to feel understood. We all want to feel valued. We all desire to be known. We all want a safe person with whom we can be entirely ourselves. For those of us who have been raised to believe that we must hide our feelings and reject expressing ourselves emotionally, life can feel like a very lonely place.

Do you ever feel alone and isolated? Do you sometimes feel that life is a long list of achievements, expectations, responsibilities, and duties? Do you come to the end of the day wishing to be understood, to be encouraged, appreciated, and seen? Do you long to be loved and accepted for exactly who you are with no questions asked and no judgments made? You are not alone. All men crave meaning in their lives.

Many of us feel that we've expended a great deal of energy each day working, breadwinning, and taking care of others only to receive little emotional support in return. A lot of times, this is because we don't know how to ask for what we need.

It's really important to let go of the expectation that we must handle everything on our own. That's a dangerous place to be. Reaching out to a partner, wife, or friend for emotional and spiritual support is one of the bravest and most noble things you can do. None of us are made to do this on our own.

Proverbs 18:24 says that "a man of many companions may come to ruin, but there is a friend who sticks closer than a brother." We need other men in our lives who are close like brothers.

Think of emotional connection as an underground spring full of fresh, clean, life-giving water. When you allow someone in your life access to your emotional well, you are able to release significant amounts of stress, be refreshed in your heart, and enjoy a freedom you'll never have when you're isolated.

— ACTION STEP —

Journal today about how you were raised as a boy and how that impacts your willingness and ability to open your heart with others.

Who sticks closer to me than a brother? Am I able to be emotionally connected and totally real with some trustworthy friends?

THE SECRET POWER OF AFFIRMATION

Have you ever thought something favorable about someone but kept your thoughts to yourself? Most of us have done so at one time or another in our lives. For some, it's our primary mode of operation. Why is that?

We may think that complimenting our kids too much may grow their egos a bit out of proportion. Or perhaps we feel that bestowing too many compliments upon our wives may foster an annoying habit of expectation. Or maybe we just find it hard to express what's in our hearts in a way that doesn't feel awkward, uncomfortable, or too touchy-feely for us.

Our primary reason for holding back on our compliments of others usually has much more to do with our fear of emotional commitment and intimacy than any swollen heads on the part of others. A good rule of thumb when it comes to affirming the people in your life? "JUST SAY IT!"

Don't keep quiet. Compliments that are genuine and come from the heart not only foster connection and deep bonding but affirm that you see the people in your life for who they are and that you recognize what matters to them. No matter if you affirm their character, their gifts, their personality, or their efforts, the time you take to express what you notice about someone will most of the time result in increased appreciation and returned affection.

Affirmations can even resolve differences and cut through relational tension.

Everyone responds to affirmation. To be seen and known is life-giving. To be affirmed for who you are is deeply encouraging to every person. Affirmation may be the greatest gift you can give someone you care about. Give it to them today!

— ACTION STEP —

Be on the lookout today for opportunities to affirm others. "JUST SAY IT."

Do I regularly affirm the people I care about in my life? What keeps me from saying what's in my heart? What people in my life can I affirm today in a way that makes them feel loved and appreciated?

THE CONSUMER

Gypsy moths are destructive creatures. They have been know to defoliate more than a million acres of U.S. forest land per year. They live to consume, and they leave damage and destruction in their path. If we're not mindful of our own selfish nature and if we don't have purposeful and meaningful targets that we're aiming for, we can look more like a gypsy moth than we might want to believe. We consume and take and even destroy for our own benefit, oftentimes at the expense of others.

When we're not meaningfully engaged in creating and cultivating for the benefit of others, then we're probably spending a lot of our time in selfish, me-first consumption. We develop a consumer-first mindset. We're looking out mainly for ourselves. With this mindset in a relationship, we become the "taker," doing what we want to do with no regard for our family or friends. In business, we can come across as competitive at all costs, arrogant, or cold. We become inwardly focused and live mainly to satisfy our own desires.

This is not authentic manhood. We see time and time again in our own stories and in the stories of other men throughout history that consumer-first living does not bring ultimate personal fulfillment. Nor is it beneficial to others. We become like human gypsy moths with an insatiable appetite for selfish consumption.

We were designed by God to be so much more than this. We were created to be givers, creators, and cultivators for the benefit of others. When we live authentically from our hearts and follow the way of Jesus, we become life-givers. We offer ourselves to others. We become concerned for the well-being of those around us. Authentic men bring a life-giving spirit to all of their relationships.

— ACTION STEP —

Pick out a person in your life and do something good for them that is life-giving. Something that is purely for their benefit and may even surprise them. Experience the joy of being a life-giver.

In what ways do I act primarily as a consumer in my life? Would others say that I bring a life-giving spirit to my relationships? To my work life? How can I develop ways to create and cultivate in my life for the benefit of others?

THE EXPERT

Just as dangerous as the selfish consumer is the self-proclaimed expert. He boasts that he has all the answers and that he rarely misses the bullseye. He spends his time critiquing others, but you never really see him play. In fact, he's oftentimes a pretender, a poser.

In business, he's the one who knows how everything should be done but declines to get involved in what it takes to do it. He's the armchair coach, the heckler in the crowd, and the excluder of those he feels don't deserve to be in his limelight. He's the "good one" in the church who shows up each Sunday to control how things are done. But when it comes time for the work, he's nowhere to be found.

The self-proclaimed expert is the guy carrying the measuring stick in his pocket wherever he goes so he can check to see who measures up to his standards of excellence. He's the self-righteous critic, the perfectionistic parent, the unreasonably demanding teacher, the authority on everything—at least he thinks so.

Maybe we all make the mistake of doing this once in a while. But it's essential to be aware of it when we do and to not let it become who we are. An authentic man who is committed to the way of Jesus does not need to critique others but is more focused on jumping in and helping where help is needed. He uses his true expertise to coach and guide others with humility and kindness, and he is always looking for opportunities to encourage others in ways that put wind in their sails.

An authentic man is a life-giver, not a life-taker . . . even with his words.

— ACTION STEP —

Be mindful today of your "measuring stick" and how you use it to critique and encourage others.

Could it be that others see me as the expert know-it-all who is always being critical? Do I wield my skills and knowledge as a weapon or offer them as a gift? How can I spend more time recognizing other's gifts and abilities rather than showcasing my own?

THE PAUSE

One of the most dynamic symbols in a piece of music is . . . the pause. Called a *fermata*, the pause is like a long, deep breath between one musical phrase and the next. It usually comes in anticipation or expectation of what is to come, that is, the entrance into a new phrase or a deeper complexity in the music.

It's much like the taking of a long and deep breath. You breathe in. Hold for a moment. And then let it out with a long sigh. In that sigh, your entire body lets go of tension, thought, and rigidity . . . and it relaxes.

You breathe in. You pause. You breathe out . . . and suddenly your soul feels more connected to your heart, to your mind, to the room, to your world . . . and if we desire it and seek it, more connected to God.

The pause provides us a way to open ourselves up and connect to God, to each other, and to ourselves. Each time we mindfully breathe in, we become more aware of the life-giving power of the Holy Spirit of Christ in us. Each time we breathe out, we release the toxic stress that confines and entraps us.

Reflect on this . . . the very first thing we do when we come into this world is take a breath. God created us with a permanent and lasting "soul connection" to Him. We carry within us the very breath of our creator. We live because God breathed life into us.

"God formed the man of dust from the ground and breathed into his nostrils the breath of life" (Genesis 2:7). God "himself gives to all mankind life and breath" (Acts 17:25). Every breath we take is a gift from and connection to God.

Take some times during your day to stop, become aware of God's presence in your life, prayerfully pause, and breathe. Reflect gratefully on every single breath He gives you.

For a man to connect at a soul level with those around him, he must first remember his soul connection with God.

Each and every day, like the *fermata* in a piece of music, simply pause. And breathe. Prayerfully take a vital step toward restoring your God-given rhythm, your moment-by-moment soul connection with God.

— ACTION STEP —

Set aside some time today to be still. Close your eyes. And breathe. Breathe deeply. Breathe slowly. Allow yourself to receive the breath of life from the Lord. Allow each breath to flood your heart with gratefulness to Him and carry that gratefulness with you as you go about your day.

Can I make time daily to pause from my busyness and stress and deeply breathe in the soul-restoring, life-giving breath of God? Can I insert prayerful "pauses" into the rhythm of my days to connect with God on a soul level?

Day Fifty

LIVING IN COMMUNITY

In today's western culture, we have learned to value independence and individualism. We fear being "needy" or "dependent" on anyone else for our well-being. While being "needy" can be an unhealthy response in a relationship, we have come to equate "needing our family and friends" with "neediness." This false equation has caused many men not only to avoid relying on others but to fear the kind of closeness they truly need.

Human beings need other human beings. God created us to be in relationships with each other and with Him. In the garden, God gave Adam and Eve relationship with each other and relationship with Him. It seems to me those relationships are the most important things He gave them.

It's in relationship that we flourish and grow. Through relationships, we nurture others while they nurture us. Relationships create an environment for us to live authentically and truthfully.

When Jesus was born into the world, He was called "Emmanuel," which means "God with us." While God has always been with us, the presence of God physically side by side with us in our created world taught us unequivocally that God values above all . . . relationships. From Genesis onward, we can see we were created to be in relationships.

Relationships represent our most natural state. Just as we need oxygen to breathe, we need relationships—our friends, our families, our communities—to truly thrive as individuals. In fact, our uniqueness as individual humans is highlighted in our relationships with others.

Of course, we remain independent and unique beings. But we bond relationally with other independent and unique beings in interdependent relationships. We need each other.

Your journey toward authentic manhood works best when you engage in community with other men, trusted brothers whom you can count on to challenge you and be there for you. Guys who will have your back and support you through thick and thin.

Make it a priority to pursue deep, dependable, and meaningful relationships with other men and truly enjoy one of the greatest gifts God has given to us . . . relationships where you can give life to others and receive it for yourself. Authentic men pursue authentic relationships.

— ACTION STEP —

Take time to reflect on the importance God places on relationships. Identify some ways you can flourish and grow in your close relationships.

Do I make it a priority to pursue deep, dependable, and meaningful relationships with other men? What fears and insecurities hold me back from investing personally and relationally in the lives of others?

LOVE LETTERS TO GOD

Pursuing authentic manhood doesn't ensure that life will always be smooth sailing. Every one of us will face significant challenges and changes along the way. During the course of our lives, we will experience not only changes in our circumstances but also changes that come with our different seasons of life. When we're twenty-three, we won't face the same problems, issues, joys, or challenges that a man of fifty-two will face. Each season of life will present us with new road signs for our journey. How we adapt to and approach each season will impact our ability to transition from one stage to another well.

Ongoing and intentional prayer can help us be mindful of transitions as life changes. It helps us stay connected to God and deepen our relationship with Him even as we move from one life stage to the next. We can pray to see things from His perspective as life unfolds for us. As the unknown becomes the known, we can pray to desire His will above our own.

King Solomon of the Old Testament models a beautiful prayer life for us. In Song of Solomon, we can read beautiful and intimate poetry written about Solomon's prayers to God. They're depicted as an intimate relationship with a wife or lover. They kind of feel like love letters to God.

Solomon is declared in scripture to be wiser than all men in his time. We can learn a lot from his letters. He mentors us in both his triumphs and his mistakes. He warns against vices and celebrated victories. He understood in a very personal way what it meant to be human, to be a man, to be faced with issues of power, responsibility, relationships, and challenges. And, throughout his life, he kept God close to his heart. He stayed connected to God by talking to Him, seeking relationship with Him and praying to Him in an ongoing and intentional way. His prayer life seems to be at the center of him becoming the wise king that we know him to have been.

Whatever season you find yourself in at this point in your life, stay connected to the heart of God by praying to Him. Talking to Him. Like Solomon, you might find it meaningful to write poetry to Him. As life happens and transitions occur, pray to see things as God sees them, as best as you can. And as you grow in your prayer, like Solomon, you'll grow in your wisdom to step into life's changes . . . and transition well.

— ACTION STEP —

Reflect on your prayer life today and your heart's connection with the heart of God.

What can we learn from how Solomon stayed connected to God? What can I regularly pray to God that will connect me with His heart?

REVERSE ENGINEERING

"Reverse engineering" is looking at the finished product so that you can discern how to create it in the first place.

The idea of "reverse engineering" can help us understand how to transition from one season of life to another well. Take a look at how other men you admire have successfully moved through their various stages of life. Learn from them. Imagine the life you want to live and who you want to be. Apply their wisdom and their experience to your journey.

We need experienced men to whom we can look for guidance and wisdom. We need mentors who can show us how it's done, to warn us of upcoming challenges and hurdles and to caution us about pitfalls, traps, and sinkholes.

When you surround yourself with men who've gone before you, you will be better equipped to pursue your own path and face whatever life throws your way. Then, later on down the road, you'll have the privilege of offering that same thing to men coming behind you.

Pursue men ahead of you who have lived life well and receive the blessing of their wisdom. And as an authentic man, be committed to offering the same for those who will be looking to you for your wisdom.

— ACTION STEP —

Identify three men you admire and who have transitioned well in their seasons of life. Ask them if they would be willing to mentor you to do the same.

Who are some older men I admire that I can learn from and who can help guide me on my journey? As I think ahead, who do I want to be in the next stages of my life?

Day Fifty-Three
THE PATH

A map is helpful when we find ourselves in unknown territory. Maps are also helpful for overall perspective in understanding where we are . . . to see what path we're on.

What path are you on in your life map? Can you see where you are? What are you heading toward? It's easy to get confused about where we're headed in life. There are so many mixed messages coming at us daily from multiple sources that promote different pathways. Many of them challenge our identity and often point us toward a more "attractive," more "manly," more culturally constructed image. It's easy to get caught up in what and where others think we should be.

Scripture gives us a map. It gives us a path that leads us to our ultimate meaning in life. It's the path to knowing Jesus as the one who came to restore God's original design in us. It's the path to know Jesus. Not just know about Him. Not just to have said a particular prayer to Him. To know Him. To know His way. To know Him personally. To know what He says to us and who He calls us to be. To know of His promises of salvation and of the abundant life. To know and receive His love and His grace. To know how He lived and treated friends and enemies. To know and receive what He's done for us.

To know Jesus means to be moving toward Him. To be sure our path is pointed toward Him. To create space in our path to spend time with Him and know His words to us. And to listen. Scripture describes knowing Jesus as eternal life.

Read a scene in scripture where Jesus is talking or serving and just be there with Him. Picture Him speaking the words to you personally. See Him look at you. Hear Him saying the words. Feel the heart behind His words and His actions. Be with Him in your mind and in your heart. Get to know Him and His way. You will become more like Him.

James 4:8 tells us that if you draw near to God, He will draw near to you. Draw near to Jesus.

— ACTION STEP —

The best way to know someone is to spend time with them. Reflect in your own life journey where you are in drawing near to Jesus.

Am I on the path toward knowing Jesus? Would creating time and space to draw near to Him help me know him better and help me be more like Him?

Day Fifty-Four

WHAT CAN I DO FOR YOU?

One of my favorite Jesus stories is recorded in Mark 10:46-52. It takes place in the city of Jericho. Jesus was with His disciples and they were leaving the city to travel to Jerusalem for the biggest event in the history of the world. So, it was a very important trip.

The crowds surrounding Jesus were large. Many people were following and wanting to get close to Him as He began the journey. A blind beggar was there, sitting on the roadside. His name was Bartimaeus. When the beggar learned that Jesus was near, he cried out and asked Jesus to have mercy on him. The crowd rebuked him and told him to be quiet. I imagine they were telling him not to get in Jesus' way. But he cried out again. Jesus stopped. Jesus called the blind man to Himself.

As Bartimaeus approached, Jesus didn't get angry at him. He didn't tell him he was in the way. He didn't tell him he was causing trouble or that he was delaying this all-important journey. Jesus simply asked him a question. He asked, "What do you want me to do for you?" Bartimaeus answered, "Let me recover my sight." He just wanted to be able to see, and he believed Jesus could heal him.

Jesus healed him. He healed him and said, "Go your way; your faith has made you well."

I love this story for a lot of reasons, but the main one is that it shows everything about the heart of Jesus. In the middle of His journey toward the event that would fulfill His ultimate purpose and would give a new hope to all of mankind, He stopped. He stopped for a blind beggar on the side of the road. He didn't preach at him or act irritated by the interruption, He just asked him what He could do for him. And then He served him.

How many times do you have opportunities to stop in your "road" of life and see the needs of others, care enough to ask how you can help, and then be there to serve? Authentic men look for opportunities to be the hands and feet of Jesus for others in need.

— ACTION STEP —

Put yourself in the shoes of the blind beggar and imagine what he must have felt when Jesus stopped and healed him. Reflect on ways you can serve others with the heart of Jesus.

How would you describe the heart of Jesus from this story? What do you think His heart is toward you?

Day Fifty-Five

GRIEF TRANSFORMATION

Hard times can bring grief. Grief can be uncomfortable. We want it to stop. We want it to end. We want to feel good again. And we want it now. And yet like a persistent storm, that rumbling deep within our souls won't end. It makes it hard for us to function, to move forward, to feel ourselves again, to connect to ourselves, our world, and others. We feel bogged down in a sea of fatigue and pain.

Most men want to slough those feelings off, to triumph over them, to stuff them down or pack them away neatly as though with a trash compactor, so that we can get back to the business of living our lives. So we can "be ourselves" again. But no matter how hard we try to master our feelings of sadness and loss, they seem to lurk over us like dark clouds.

When a storm hits, the skies don't always turn sunny blue the next day. It runs its course. It leaves destruction and sorrow in its wake. It brings with it clouds and torrents of rain, sometimes for days and weeks to come. You can't rush nature. And you can't rush grief.

But this is what you can do. You can trust the words of Jesus. He assures us that God will not abandon us in our times of grief (Matthew 5:4).

111

You can be assured that God won't abandon you, and then you can allow grief to do its work in you. This is where you grow. This is where you mature. Like Jonah, in the belly of the whale, this is where you can let go and meet God as your most real and raw self. You can take your grief and sadness to Him. You can take your heart to Him. This is where you need Him the most. In the dark night of your soul.

This is where true transformation is most likely to take place . . . when we meet God in our depths . . . when we give it all to Him. It's where we learn to let go and trust. This unwanted grief can become one of the most meaningful and character-shaping chapters of your life . . . if you invite Him into it with you.

— ACTION STEP —

Reflect in your journal how grief has helped shape the man you are today. Is there any grief you need to invite God into with you?

What grief or pain have you felt in life that has knocked you down and out? Have you tried to bury it and move on? What if you sat in it with your Creator, the One who promises not to abandon you in your pain?

THE SEASON OF SPRING

Living out our authentic manhood well hinges in some part on our ability to know what season of life we're in, what needs to be prioritized in that season, and what opportunities and threats that season presents. Life is more than just living day-to-day. It's made up of back-to-back-to-back seasons of life.

Think of the first season of a man's life as spring. This season is all about a man coming to terms with his identity. This season generally lasts into a young man's early twenties, when a boy becomes a man. An important key to this stage is that he transitions well. This is when a boy is usually making a break from the home he grew up in. He takes a job or he goes to college or he joins the military or he assumes some new responsibility. But during this time of transition, he must grow up.

This is a season when life finally stares a man in his face. He is no longer just living under the wing of mom and dad. To thrive, he must transition into manhood.

The main questions he must begin to answer in this season are: "Who am I?" and "Who am I not?" Will he be satisfied with being big or little; musical or mechanical; athletic or academic; will he be satisfied with being introverted or extroverted; handsome or plain? He must wrestle with his identity. Coming to terms with both his talents and limitations is important in this season.

It's also the time in life for a man to accept himself as God has made him. This will allow him to look ahead and plan his way and not get caught up in wishing away his life.

This will be his first season to pursue Jesus as a man and not a boy. He learns to live his life in the joy and hope of knowing Him. It's a good season to learn that, despite the struggles and the fears, life is a gift from God meant to be savored, honored, and enjoyed. That life is about more than just his successes, his wealth, his fame, or his achievements. He can learn to serve and give life to others.

If a young man lives in these ways in his spring season, he will begin his journey wisely and will set the course for a life of meaning, passion, and purpose.

— ACTION STEP —

Answer the big questions of the spring season.

Who am I? Who am I not?

Day Fifty-Seven

THE SEASON OF SUMMER

Let's call a man's twenties and thirties his season of summer. The twenties should be the first adult stage of a man's life. The first part of this season is about learning, and with it comes some real threats and dangers. For a lot of guys in their twenties there is danger that they will get lost in an extended period of adolescence and pursue boyish behaviors indefinitely—in effect, to never grow up. Extended adolescence can derail a young man in his pursuit of authentic manhood.

Another danger that applies especially to a man in his twenties is his sexual energy. This is the season in which he can decide if his sexual energy is going to dominate him, or if he's going to use it in a principled manner. He determines if passion is going to be something he uses or if it uses and controls him. That's an important question for a man to answer in this season of his life.

There are also major opportunities in this summer season, and maybe the greatest one is the opportunity to learn, learn, learn. He will take his first career steps . . . maybe his first real job. He will make his first professional mistakes and be able to learn from them. This is a season to prioritize learning and development over all other variables so he can set the stage for his career. This is the time to take risks and seize opportunities.

115

The second half of summer season is in a man's thirties. This is where he hones in on a vocation. His thirties are where he begins growing and building from things he's learned in his twenties. This is a season of growth. This is the time to perfect his skill set . . . to start logging hours in his craft . . . to begin distinguishing himself and understanding how he adds value to society.

Many men in their thirties begin families. As wonderful as this is, it can bring some unique challenges that he hasn't experienced. With additional demands on his time and the pressure to provide, life can become more stressful and busy. He may be tempted to let his work/life balance get out of whack and even get disconnected from God. He can be tempted to neglect important, character-shaping relationships with other men. It can feel like a struggle to keep his head above water.

A key word to remember in this season is margin. A man needs to learn to create margin in the middle of all of the good pursuits of family, work, friends, and play so he can gracefully move in and out of those important areas. Without margin, the first thing that gets compromised is relationships. Authentic relationships require time. Without margin, it's not going to happen.

Some of the key questions for a man's season of summer include: What do I want out of life? Where will I distinguish myself professionally? How am I different from my parents? What do I really believe? Around what person or conviction will I organize my life? How do I prioritize the demands on my life?

— ACTION STEP —

Answer the big questions of this season.

What do I want out of life? What do I really believe?

Day Fifty-Eight
THE SEASON OF FALL

The season of fall is where a man transitions out of the early adulthood of his twenties and thirties into the fall season of life. This is the season of influence, generally from age forty to age sixty. There can be a great harvest in this season from the seeds a man has sown and cultivated in the spring and summer of his life.

During this transition from summer to fall, a man typically evaluates his successes and failures from the last twenty years. Has he achieved everything he wanted? Does he have dreams that remain unfulfilled? Can his mistakes be redeemed? Are his accomplishments really that fulfilling? If he doesn't come to terms with all these things, then the great harvest of his influence may suffer.

Men who don't transition well into middle adulthood usually fall to the major threat of this season—a mid-life crisis. He feels restless, maybe because of unfulfilled dreams or regrets he believes can't be resolved. It typically plays itself out with guys turning to escapes to numb the pain or making futile attempts to relive their youthful years.

To transition well in this season a man needs vision and hope. He needs to remember that God put him on this earth to create and cultivate. He needs to be clear about what he's passionate about and what his purpose is in life.

The great opportunity in this season of life can be summed up in one word: *influence*. It is in this season that a man can be more powerful and productive than he ever has been before. It is in this season that he's on center stage. Daniel Levinson calls men between the ages of forty-five and sixty the "dominant generation." He says that the guys in this season create and implement the governing ideas in every sector of society—whether it's politics, business, religion, art, or science.

Hopefully a man in this stage has reached a certain level of influence. He very well could be positioned to make a bigger impact for God and His Kingdom in this season than at any other season in his life so far. With his age and experience, he has the incredible opportunity to be a positive influence.

— ACTION STEP —

Answer the big questions of this season.

What dreams or hopes do I feel have gone unfulfilled in my life? What can I change now to put me on the path I want to be on? Am I being a positive influence on others around me?

THE SEASON OF WINTER

A man's sixties and beyond are generally considered to be his winter season of life. This is the sage season. It's in this season that a man should be marked by wisdom, experience, and respect. That's what "sage" implies. Proverbs 20:29 says, "The glory of young men is their strength, but the splendor of old men is their gray hair." There's more to that than just the color of a man's hair! His composure, his maturity, and his insight should distinguish him.

In this season of life a man is not perceived by younger men as a competitor as much as he is perceived as a sage who is qualified to coach them in their life journeys. Many men in this season possess the confidence necessary to bless younger men by sharing openly with them about their failures as well as their successes.

If you were to imagine manhood as a game, this season would involve a man repositioning himself from the role of star player to that of a coach. Instead of being cheered for, he finds himself cheering for, coaching, and encouraging the success of the younger men around him. Only men who've continued to grow and mature in their faith can attain the level of selflessness necessary to assume this strategic position from the sidelines, thus experiencing the ultimate finish in life that God desires for us to have.

The greatest danger of this season is for a man to buy the lie that he can no longer contribute. He's got to realize that although he may be retiring from his career, he is not being released from his calling to invest in other men. It's important to remember he's not being put out to pasture and that he can make his greatest contributions at this stage in life.

This is the ultimate season for creating and cultivating by blessing others. Oftentimes, this is when a man has more freedom than he's ever had before and can possibly direct his creative energy where he pleases. He can pour into younger generations. He can use his wisdom to create and guide projects that will have a positive impact in a community and make a difference in the world. This is the prime season for a man to multiply his influence.

The journey toward authentic manhood has challenges in every phase of life. But the fulfillment, satisfaction, and purpose that a man experiences when he knows who he is and whose he is by far outweighs all of the challenges combined.

— ACTION STEP —

Answer the big question for this last season.

What do I want to contribute in this season of my life?

A LIFE-GIVING SPIRIT

"To everything there is a season, and a time for every purpose under heaven, a time to give birth and a time to die, a time to plant and a time to uproot, a time to kill and a time to heal, a time to tear down and a time to build up" (Ecclesiastes 3:1-3). Each part of a man's life holds different surprises, expectations, challenges, and seasons.

We will have seasons of gain and seasons of loss . . . seasons of planting and seasons of harvesting . . . seasons of learning and seasons of teaching . . . seasons of success and seasons of failure . . . seasons of birth and seasons of death. Life seems to be designed around different seasons.

What this makes clear is that life will have its ups and downs. Good times and bad times. Enjoyable times and challenging times. A lot of those things are beyond our control. But what we can control is who we are choosing to be in each of these seasons.

We can choose to be a *life-taker*, where we suck the life out of every room, where we see the worst in every person and situation, and where we're simply focused on our own selfish desires. Or we can choose to be a *life-giver*, where we give life to others, where we try to see the best in every person and situation, and where we are thinking about the needs of others.

No matter the season, our most meaningful joy will come from the purpose we find in giving life to others. Sure, sometimes what we plant may never sprout. But there's nothing like giving life to someone else . . . to help them out . . . to meet them where they are . . . to love them through the good and the bad.

It's what Jesus calls us to do. He tells us to love one another as He loves us (John 15:12). He tells us to give life to others as He gives life to us!

The way of authentic manhood is the way of Jesus . . . to be a life-giving spirit to others.

— ACTION STEP —

Reflect on the spirit you carry into every relationship and every situation. Spend some time journaling on ways you would like to be a life-giver to others.

Do I choose to be a life-giver, following the way of Jesus in all circumstances? Am I focused mostly on my own pleasure or also on giving life to others?

SCAN HERE to learn more about Invite Press, a premier publishing imprint created to invite people to a deeper faith and living relationship with Jesus Christ.

Printed in the USA
CPSIA information can be obtained
at www.ICGtesting.com
LVHW042100100224
771306LV00009B/1324